Beyond the Textbook

Beyond the Textbook

Teaching History Using Documents and Primary Sources

David Kobrin

Heinemann
Portsmouth, NH

Heinemann
A division of Reed Elsevier Inc.
361 Hanover Street
Portsmouth, NH 03801–3912

Offices and agents throughout the world

Some of the material in this work has appeared previously in the following articles. They are used here with permission.

David Kobrin, "It's My Country, Too: A Proposal for a Student Historian's History of the United States," *Teachers College Record*, Volume 94, Number 2, Winter 1992, pp. 329–342. Copyright © by Teachers College, Columbia University.

David Kobrin, Ed Abbott, John Ellinwood, and David Horton, "Learning History by Doing History," *Educational Leadership*, April, 1993, pp. 39–41.

David Kobrin, "Let the Future Write the Past: Classroom Collaboration, Primary Sources, and the Making of High School Historians," *The History Teacher*, Volume 28, Number 4, August, 1995.

Work on this book has been supported in part by an individual grant (94–120) from the National Historical Publications and Records Commission, National Archives.

Acknowledgments for borrowed material can be found on page 97.

Library of Congress Cataloging-in-Publication Data

Kobrin, David, 1941–
    Beyond the textbook : teaching history using documents and primary sources / David Kobrin.
      p. cm.
    Includes bibliographical references.
    ISBN: 0-435-08880-7 (alk. paper)
    1. History—Study and teaching (Higher)—United States.
I. Title.
D16.3.K64   1996
907.1′173—dc20   96-406
                                     CIP

Editor: Carolyn Coman
Production: Vicki Kasabian
Book design: Jenny Jensen Greenleaf
Cover design: Studio Nine

Printed in the United States of America on acid-free paper
07 06   VP   12 13

Contents

This book is for my loving wife, Diane, who is beyond the textbook

Acknowledgments

First and foremost, I want to acknowledge the cooperation of those teachers who willingly allowed me to work with them, including teaching in their classrooms: Ed Abbott, Jim Charleson, the late Nick Christopher, John Ellinwood, Chris Hayes, David Horton, Albin Moser, Brenda Rudman, and Peter Waddington. And then there is a long list of teachers, teacher educators, student teachers, administrators, and researchers who took the time to read all, or parts, of my manuscript in various stages of its development. I am grateful to all these readers for their suggestions, and for the care that they took with my words and ideas: Ed Abbott, Scott Barr, Louis Barrassi, Jonathan Bassett, Diane Berreth, Orah Bilmes, Gail Borod, Ron Brandt, James Coughlin, John Duffy, Mike Eckenroth, John Ellinwood, Beth Havercamp, Jeremy Kaplan, Robert D. Kuklis, Joe McDonald, Lynn Murray, James Percoco, Wynell Schamel, John Anthony Scott, Elma Shannon, Peter Waddington, Pat Wasley, Herb Woodell, John Zilboorg, and my good friend Bill Zimmerman. Wynell Schamel and Beth Havercamp of the National Archives were especially helpful and supportive over a period of many months. John Anthony Scott and John Duffy, both associated with the American Historical Association's Committee on History in the Classroom, provided insightful feedback.

I also want to thank Joyce Stevos and the Providence School Department for their support of various projects in the Providence schools. Carolyn Coman, Roberta Lew, and Vicki Kasabian, at Heinemann, were always professional and friendly. And, finally, an individual grant from the National

Historical Publications and Records Commission supported my work during 1994–1995. I am grateful for the funds the grant provided and for the helpful attitude of Kathy Jacob and other staff members.

Preface

One of the wonderful aspects of my job in the teacher education program at Brown University is that it allows me to work collaboratively with teachers in the Providence, Rhode Island, public schools. Each year I spend between one-quarter and one-half of my time in urban schools. That has given me an opportunity to develop working relationships with history and social studies teachers and their students. For six years, what the classroom teachers and I have done is to plan and then coteach units and yearlong courses that asked students to use primary sources to study history, whether of nineteenth-century America or the Renaissance, just as if they were themselves historians.

The schools we worked in were diverse. They included an academic magnet school with an entrance exam, where more than 90 percent of the graduating students went on to four-year colleges, as well as three other schools with a high proportion of recent immigrants and mainstreamed ESL students, a majority of young people from economically disadvantaged families and a highly transient student population. Actual daily absentee rates in many classes ran above 25 percent.

Our classroom experiences were mixed. We were not always successful according to our own or the students' standards. It took time to learn, for instance, what was necessary so that mainstreamed ESL students, or native-born students who test below "grade level," could read and understand complicated source materials, or why students who care little about school in general, and have a history of frustration and failure in school, would decide to work seriously as student historians, analyzing materials, generating appropriate questions, searching for patterns, and validating all statements by specific references to primary sources.

Over time, clear patterns emerged. *Beyond the Textbook: Teaching History Using Documents and Primary Sources* is about what we learned from our successes as well as our mistakes. After six years of brainstorming ideas, teaching collaboratively with highly experienced teachers as well as those early in their careers, discussing lesson plans, units, and curricula for yearlong courses, evaluating student work, and assessing feedback from students, I feel I can draw five main conclusions:

1. With few exceptions, mainstreamed students are capable of working as student historians with primary sources; that is, actually constructing the history they study.
2. Success requires that students care about their work as student historians for reasons of their own, which *they* have developed for themselves, even when it would be more efficient for teachers to tell them why they should care (Chapter 2).
3. Students need each other; they must learn to work collaboratively (Chapter 3).
4. The best way for students to develop the skills, habits, and attitudes they need is by following "simple rules," which can serve as guidelines to using documents and writing histories even in unforeseen situations. Students learn skills *while* they are engaged as student historians (Chapter 4).
5. For students to develop higher-level thinking skills requires an evaluation and grading "structure" that prompts and encourages each of them to go through a process of learning and practicing how to think and solve problems (Chapter 5).

Chapters 1 and 6 provide a frame for the rest of the book: Chapter 1 offers a starting point by looking at the teaching of history and suggesting why change is necessary; Chapter 6 discusses a possible future course, based on the use of documents and primary sources, and its implications.

For many classroom teachers, theories about how to teach may not be enough. Interesting ideas can get us only so far until they are tried and tested in classrooms. This is one reason why *Beyond the Textbook* also includes accounts of actual classroom lessons to illustrate, support, and amplify the ideas discussed. Some of the examples feature sample handouts and primary sources, and, where helpful, excerpts from student writing. Although the classroom samples are meant to form a bridge between espoused theory and actual practice, these records of our experience in high schools are not intended as models to be copied. Their purpose is twofold: to offer nuanced illustrations of what student historian "theory" looks like when translated into classroom practice, and, in so doing, to help teachers discover approaches, methods, and techniques that might work in their own classrooms.

My hope is that the descriptions of lessons and the accompanying discussions will prompt teachers to think about what might be useful to them, with their students, when they teach history and social studies. The classroom examples are intended as catalysts for renewed reflection about teaching.

This book was written with the special needs of history and social studies teachers, curriculum planners, teacher educators, and preservice teachers, grades seven through twelve, in mind. Questions about history and the teaching of history dominate the book. For example: Why rely on documents and other primary sources to learn history when good, up-to-date textbooks are readily available? What can teachers do to get students who barely care about school to care about being student historians? How do students learn the complex skills and attitudes required to work as student historians? How can teachers find time in an already overloaded day to weigh the merits of diverse approaches to teaching history?

These questions and others like them also have broader applications. They are particular examples of larger questions that are generic to teaching and learning, no matter what the subject: How much do textbooks dictate the curriculum? What is needed to involve students in their school work? How are higher-level thinking skills mastered? How do teachers continue to develop their professional skills? The problems, issues, and questions raised and discussed should be of interest to those for whom teaching and learning—and teachers and students—are important.

1
Constructing History

WORKING WITH OTHERS

The professional development session for teachers takes place over pizza, soft drinks, and beer in the late afternoon of a typical school day. By choice we are meeting at Casserta's Pizzeria, arguably the best in Providence. There are no building administrators or district representatives present, only classroom teachers and myself, a faculty member in a teacher education program. No one has told us that we *must* be there, nor has anyone granted us special permission to meet. It is not clear who is in charge. Our agenda, in addition to sharing pizza together, is to see who would like to co-operate in designing classroom projects to improve the teaching of history in the city's schools. The principal question we wind up asking is: What must teachers do so that mainstreamed students can learn history by working from primary sources?[1]

We are an example of a self-motivated professional development team that relies more on teacher initiative than on administrative directives, policy mandates, or national consensus. We believe—although we are far from using such language with one another—that the future does not have to be in place for teachers to do their part. Even in schools where difficult working conditions leave little time for reflection, something can be accomplished.

The five of us—four history/social studies teachers from three city public schools and myself—have come together for reasons of our own. Each teacher lingers over pizza and conversation only as long as he wants. And the collaboration formalized this afternoon continues only as long as each partner believes it worth the time and effort on top of already crowded teaching days. For some around the table that will mean one or two student historian projects over the next several months. For others, including teachers who become involved after hearing about student historian work in their building, the result is six years of ongoing classroom experiment.

This book is about changes that teachers and students can initiate in their own classrooms, and why their participation is necessary. Teachers are powerful, more so than they often realize. They are the fulcrum; change will only come when they actively will it. I believe that classroom teachers hold the key to meaningful progress because they alone among professional educators are in there with the kids every day. They alone must know not only their subject matter but what the students in their classrooms need in order to learn—*and* they must practice daily what they preach. Professional teachers best understand the complex realities of the settings where teaching and learning take place.

Despite the value we placed on individual teaching styles, we found that we initiated projects and made progress more easily when we worked together. Over six years of continuing effort, including two-week units, yearlong history courses, and projects that brought diverse students from two schools together to critique each other's "histories," the single most important variable enabling us to succeed was collaboration. We formed a partnership within the school that extended beyond the school.

Because my university-based teacher education position required me to work in the city's public schools one-quarter to one-half time, the teachers and I had resources that teachers working by themselves normally lack. When we needed photocopies, for example, I could legitimately make them at the university, a boon in schools where reliable copying machines were a scarce commodity. When we needed collections of primary sources on a particular topic, the university's resources, including advice from knowledgeable specialists in the history department, were added to what the schools had available. Furthermore, I had the freedom to leave one school and enter another largely at my own discretion—something that was rarely possible during the eight years I taught high school full-time—which facilitated connections among teachers and administrators at several schools. And, finally, after all the meetings, brainstorming, and revising of lessons, about half the time there were two teachers working together and cooperating in the same classroom.

Much to their credit, the Providence School Department supported this arrangement without dictating what we were to accomplish. This meant that I had an opportunity to develop working relationships. Just as in more personal relationships, building trust required time. With his permission, I watched one teacher teach a U.S. history class once a week, during the same period, for more than a month. Sometimes afterwards, we would talk about what had happened in those classes. Sometimes during class he would ask me to participate. But it was only after he had invited me to teach his students, observed my class, and critiqued my work that we crossed a threshold. Then we were in the same boat, ready to learn from each other's skills, expertise, and experience.

To some teachers, even in middle schools where team teaching is more common, such successful cooperative planning and teaching may seem unusual. Yet across this large nation in middle and high schools we are currently enjoying a ground swell in attention to teaching methods that either require collaboration or at least are more effective when not done in isolation from colleagues. In history and social studies, many of these projects require that students learn to analyze documents, primary sources, and artifacts. These projects include oral histories, family histories, and local histories that emulate the *Foxfire* approach; the creation of "youth archives" and student-generated immigrant histories; historical site research; the use of document packets and CD-ROMs, like those offered by the National Archives, that let student historians "construct" history in their own classrooms (I will say more about what it means to "construct" history later in this chapter); publication of student papers in "scholarly" journals designed especially for students; and such traditional standbys as the document-based questions on Advanced Placement exams.[2] The National Center for History in the Schools at UCLA also offers primary source materials and sample lessons showing how to use them.

Such cooperative projects, however, if they require dusting off little-used teaching methods, locating primary sources, or establishing fresh relationships with colleagues in the building, can seem daunting. And, in fact, they *are* often problem plagued, especially in the early stages! Yet working by yourself is also a two-edged sword. The closed classroom door grants an autonomy that many teachers have come to value, even love. But seclusion can make a teacher feel alone and powerless. With five classes and more than a hundred students a day, as well as a host of clerical responsibilities and so many in the building who can interrupt their work, teachers need to find support somewhere. Relying on an approved textbook often seems the ready answer.

BEYOND THE TEXTBOOK

Most middle and high school social studies teachers value the support a good textbook can provide.[3] Just the thought of doing without a text can be scary. After all, textbooks serve as a principal source of information in many classrooms. Especially now, with the explosion of information through technologies like CD-ROM and the Internet, and with the growing emphasis on multiculturalism and global studies, there is so much to know, one teacher can find it difficult to master everything that is expected. Textbooks offer sidebars, pictures, graphics, excerpts from primary sources, and review and discussion questions. Teacher's editions make suggestions about how to teach and how to test. And the textbook publishers gladly supply auxiliary materials, such as sample lessons, worksheets, and test questions.

Yet despite their obvious value and almost universal acceptance, textbooks have big problems. Even their staunchest advocates recognize that there is much that needs attention. For our purposes, we do not have to take sides either defending or attacking. Merely examining textbooks as a genre reveals much about how history's subject matter is written and how that affects the learning of history, and this raises important questions for those who teach history to middle and high school students: Is the history presented in textbooks "accurate"? Who writes textbooks, and why? For teachers and students, what is lost and what is gained by relying on a textbook?

Historians writing textbooks for schoolchildren have not always claimed accuracy as their primary objective. Before the founding of the American Historical Association and the professionalization of history as a discipline in the decade of the 1890s, many popular textbook authors valued the past as a source of "moral" lessons for American youth. Authors willingly repeated "misinformation" or even created "fantasized anecdotes" in order to drive their points home. Not until the 1890s and the new emphasis on "objectivity" did modern texts begin to speak in a voice that led young readers and their teachers to believe that what they had learned was *the* unchanging truth about the past.[4]

Although a tone of authority pervades textbook narratives, producing history textbooks has always been, and remains, susceptible to contemporary pressures. Like the history of curriculum development in general, the interpretations and content in history textbooks more often reflect social and cultural factors at the time of writing—factors like current political upheavals, the role of pressure groups, changing school populations, and the authors' ideology—than advances in knowledge about the subject. What district today would adopt an "objective" textbook from the 1890s? We would consider it hopelessly "out of date." Textbook accounts of Reconstruction after the Civil War offer a more poignant example. Over the course of several generations the description of Reconstruction in textbooks has changed from one of a disaster hurtful to "Southerners" to a "Second American Revolution" that valued civil over property rights. This dramatic adjustment in textbook understanding of a historical period reflects not so much the reality of the nineteenth-century past as the continuing twentieth-century redefinition of who should rightfully be included in U.S. history. Until the 1960s, blacks were virtually invisible in most U.S. history texts, except as slaves.[5]

Marketing and the business demands of publishing also intrude on the creation of textbooks. According to the American Textbook Council, the teaching of U.S. history at the secondary level is "locked-up" by ten to fifteen books, which dominate the market. The situation is similar for textbooks in other areas of history. In the judgment of the Textbook Council, this is equivalent to a "national curriculum" established *de facto* by the publishing industry. Furthermore, the historians listed as authors on the title page of texts rarely act as more than senior consultants. The actual writing, including hundreds of editorial revisions, is often done by in-house managing editors, including marketing and design personnel. Study questions and the teacher's text are usually written by anonymous writers in "development companies" who often have no special expertise in the field.[6]

Despite these ongoing difficulties, in the eyes of most students (and many teachers) their textbook appears to be an "accurate" and "complete" narrative chronology of the past. This, for me, is the central problem with textbooks: they make students think there is only one true and accurate account of the past, which everyone should be learning.

It is important to keep in mind that textbooks as a genre are not the enemy. Chapter 6, for instance, describes a plan for a history textbook that would help middle and high school students learn *how* to learn U.S. history by studying primary sources. And, to offer a dramatic example from real life, in the 1960s students and teachers at Tougaloo and Millsaps colleges, dissatisfied with the approach to Mississippi's history in the only state-approved textbook, decided to write their own account. They wanted a description of Mississippi's past that recognized and took pride in the presence of African Americans, an account that did not skip over the state's racial conflicts. It took a court action brought by the NAACP Legal Defense and Educational Fund to add the finished product, *Mississippi: Conflict and Change,* to the state's list of approved history texts. Even then, approval did not mean adoption.[7]

Writing their textbook, however, did get students and teachers actively involved in their own learning of history in a way no conventional course could match. It is a response to the problem of textbooks worth thinking about. The students and their professors created a new history of their state and the people who lived there, a history made, they believed, for themselves and for all Mississippians. The creation of *Mississippi: Conflict and Change* is an example of "constructing" history as a way of learning history.

CONSTRUCTING HISTORY

In Charles Dickens' classic story, *A Christmas Carol*, when Scrooge is first startled by the Ghost of Christmas Past he asks the apparition in his bedroom, "Long past?"

"No. Your past," the Spirit replies with some delight at Scrooge's naïveté.

Anyone who has hung around grades seven through twelve for a while knows that history is the study of the past. But it is no longer a naive question to ask whose past? or who decides?

Defining history as a field of study, especially deciding what is to be included, what left out, and how it is all to be presented to students, is a complicated, value-laden problem that teacher-historians face on a daily basis. Teachers cannot put the history of the whole world into their students' heads. In order to be accessible, the past must be reduced. Even if an all-inclusive account were possible—which, of course, it is not—it would be unusable. There is no way around the dilemma: from what they know teachers must construct usable accounts they consider accurate and valuable for their students and themselves.

Reducing and reconstructing history in the classroom is inevitable; otherwise, teachers would be shortchanging their students. History teachers are historians whose everyday work includes connecting living students and the past. I remember teaching the First World War with a tenth-grade class. When U.S. troops finally arrived in force we ended the fighting and took the Allied leaders off to some quite posh peace tables at Versailles (1919). Germany, accepting surrender, awaited judgment from the nations who had been victorious in this barbaric war. Thinking the Versailles Conference a reasonable place to leave off the war for the moment, I went back to "pick up" the Bolshevik Revolution. I believed it was best presented as a separate subject. All was fine on the comprehension front until it came time for Lenin to plead terms for Russia's surrender to Germany at Brest-Litovsk (1918). At least half the class became terribly upset! How could that be? they wanted to know. Russia could not surrender to Germany, they said. Germany had lost the war; Germany was the loser, not the winner.

The shock that came from my failure to organize—that is, to reduce and simplify—history so that it made sense to my students, forced me to face how much of my job as a teacher involved constructing an understandable past. The consequences for school-age children are very real, which is why so much energy and polemic are invested in who controls not only the interpretations but the "boundaries" of the history presented in schools. Consider an example that paints with broad strokes. In most textbooks and school histories there is a consensus that the nation's origins lie with the

English-speaking, predominantly Protestant peoples who settled the east coast of the continent in the seventeenth century. Yet also valid is a view that stresses its Spanish speaking and African origins in the east and southwest, including what once was Mexico. The oldest church in continuous existence in the United States, built by Spanish missionaries and their Indian "servants," stands in Santa Fe, New Mexico. Clearly each of these two viewpoints presents a different sense of who "we" are—or should be—today.

Whether we are talking about the content coverage of textbooks, national standards for teaching history, or July Fourth rhetoric, then, defining history is not simply an academic question. Whoever gets to control the definition of the past has moral and political power in the present. "Stories" are one way the adult world passes its culture on to the next generation. As the formal, adult presentation of what the world is and was, history does this intentionally. Since schoolchildren and young adults are preeminently the age groups working on developing identities, the his- and her-stories taught in school become raw material for students in figuring out who their people were and how they fit into *the* story. To return to the question of "our" nation's origins, there is a big difference between learning in school that I own a place in the sun and learning that I inherit the view from the sidelines.

California's experience with social studies curriculum reform and textbook revision is an illuminating example of how intensely people care about the history children learn. Those who felt that their people or culture had been slighted or misunderstood by the revised history and social studies frameworks found opportunities to speak with determination and energy. Spokespeople for blacks, Muslims, Jews, Hispanics, and homosexuals, among others, complained about "omissions, inaccuracies, and misrepresentations" in the books under consideration. Nor did they want their past explained through someone else's perspective. One member of the state curriculum panel argued with some intensity that "to have a fifth-grade book tell children that the United States is a nation of immigrants and Native Americans are the first immigrants and Africans were forced immigrants takes the European model of immigration and tries to fit everyone else in it." Supporters of the approved text replied, in turn, that protesters were "asking for something no single book could accomplish: a separate ethnic history of their own culture or religion." Another advocate of the selected texts added that such a work would require a book "the size of the Manhattan telephone directory."[8]

Obviously, teachers cannot ask students to lug huge texts home every night to ensure a mythical inclusiveness that satisfies all. Even as technological advances make notebook computers more accessible, who could read, never mind retain, a history text as dense as the Manhattan phone book? Including "everybody" and every version of "all that happened" in a course of study is not the answer, even if it were possible. But, then, who is to be left out, and why?

To interpret history means to make decisions about who and what we call "history" and the extent to which a shared "history" is, well, shared. As long as history is thought of as a set body of information, someone will be stuck with deciding what to emphasize and what to omit. No matter who does the defining, a lot of "others" are going to be dissatisfied, and nowadays, for better and worse, they are not going to keep their feelings to themselves.

What is changing is not the nature of the problems—these tensions have always been there—but that more and more people in and out of schools recognize the consequences. Thinking seriously about how history is created means accepting the view that valid, sometimes contradictory, multiple perspectives are unavoidable. The reality of life is that the past is always presented to us via someone's writing; historians are writers. Actually, the process is compound. Historians' writings are based largely on the written sources of other writers, most of whom lived at the time they describe. Delivered history comes packaged and the shape of the package depends on someone's perceptions and the decisions that followed about what to include and omit, the best wrapping paper, how to tie the bow. An actual "past" surely existed, but the "history" we get is constructed by living and thinking historians.[9] In this sense, history can be thought of as a conversation between the past and the present: all histories are based on systematic (and therefore arguable) exclusions.

Because these understandings about the "political" nature of history are so widespread and, as we have seen, often so heartfelt, the grounds upon which certain groups have authoritatively claimed to represent all others have been seriously shaken. We are in the midst of a conceptual earthquake. Upsetting as it may be to teachers—and to parents and politicians—who do not want a fundamental upheaval in how they have always viewed the subject (and the country) they love, there is no longer a single account that all history teachers, historians, parents, and students accept as definitive.

Such a statement does not mean that, suddenly, all approaches are equally valid. Far from it! It is, instead, a recognition that recapturing the past is a value-laden act, no matter who the teacher or historian, or how pure their intentions. Like it or not, middle and high school history teachers are all "political players" in their own classrooms. The more we care about our work, the more actively involved we are in the ongoing struggle to shape history and the teaching of history.

There is so much, nowadays, that is in motion in the world of the history teacher. Students, schools, neighborhoods, methods, even historical scholarship is changing. And all those questions have become politically sensitive issues that are argued, sometimes loudly, in public. Does this mean that history teachers also must change, no matter what their past experience or their views?

CHANGE, SPACE, AND PRIVACY

In my experience, change—personal emotional and intellectual adjustment—does not come easily. It is normal, after all, to hesitate before throwing away something it has taken considerable effort to accomplish. If this book is to be helpful to teachers and students it must respect the seriousness with which we all resist change. I know this from my own teaching experiments in high school classrooms. When an experienced teacher and a student teacher and I introduced a yearlong "project-based" U.S. history course to the teacher's tenth-grade class—the entire course was packed into seven student-centered projects, all introduced in the first weeks—the class marshaled its considerable adolescent wisdom and brought work first to a crawl, then to a virtual standstill. The course was simply too large a leap from what the students were used to.

The urge to stay where we are is human. The more difficult the teaching environment, the more likely all of us will hold dear the elaborated version of teaching and learning that gets us through the days, weeks, and years. Yet for teachers to stay where they are, whatever their level of achievement in the classroom or years of working with students, is to lose ground. Mastering the craft of teaching is a lifelong process. Statements like these may sound like banalities, but if so it is because their simple wisdom is pragmatic. Change is a learning process for all those involved—unless the "change" is merely a passive acceptance of another's demands. To teach well requires attention to the ideas and practices of other professionals. It requires space and time, often *much* space and time, and sometimes privacy. Change must be personalized. Changes are not best made merely for the sake of changing.

In order to initiate change, most people first need to express their beliefs, feelings, experiences, and concerns: When the intellectual "space" where you are now is not acknowledged, it is hard to move toward a different future. If your ideas are challenged, even if only by arguments on paper, you may well feel undermined.

What is the best way to think through an idea, to consider moving from where you are now to somewhere else?

Discussions can be useful, but too often, rather than open up participants to new notions, they become a debate in which opposing views are like serves in a tennis match: they are something to be returned successfully.

The result is a discussion that solidifies where everyone already was. Questions that prompt reflection, posed in the privacy of a book, on the other hand, allow space and time for ideas to evolve in private and develop unimpeded. You may have used this technique in a workshop or in your own classroom. *In this book, the purpose of such questions is always to explore what you think without feeling "ownership" of the ideas.* The questions become a toolbox that, when used, can provide the reader with room. At their best, they allow a place to hesitate, to air concerns, to sound out a new idea. You can be unsure, even self-contradictory, without embarrassment. Your "answers" do not have to be "right." You can skip the questions you are not ready for now and come back to them later. Nor should you feel any pressure, any expectation, to accept new ideas in their entirety.

The questions in this chapter are divided into two parts. First are a set of "Assertions" intended as a warm-up activity. These are followed immediately by "Here I Stand," which provides a chance to stake out your current position as a history/social studies teacher.

ASSERTIONS: A "WARM-UP" ACTIVITY

Assertions are definitive-sounding statements. They express clear-cut points of view. The five assertions presented here are about teachers, students, textbooks, history, and the teaching of history. I chose them because they tend toward the controversial. Their purpose, then, is to raise issues. Reacting to controversial assertions can encourage clarity, especially for those teachers who, given the daily demands of teaching, may not have focused on these questions recently.

It will be difficult to agree or disagree with *all* of any of these comments. The best approach is to isolate those parts of each assertion you agree with or those you cannot accept.

Assertion 1: About Teachers

With the post-Sputnik education reforms, kids are supposed to learn by becoming active inquirers, rather than passive recipients. Yet teachers are given so-called "teacher-proof" curriculum under the assumption that reform has to be from the top down. In other words, unlike their students, teachers are not capable of being active learners but have to continue as passive recipients of someone else's knowledge.[10]

❖ *Are there parts of this assertion that you agree with?*

❖ *What do you disagree with?*

❖ *Do you have other comments you wish to make?*

Assertion 2: About Students

". . . Those are terrific kids."

"The best. Sometimes it takes them a while to let the goodness come out and take over from the darkness and suspicion they have when they come here. But inside they're all like that."

"I see why a person might devote his life to this work."[11]

❖ *Are there parts of this assertion that you agree with?*

❖ *What do you disagree with?*

❖ *Do you have other comments you wish to make?*

Assertion 3: About Textbooks

"A good text makes it possible for the student to see (or at least sense) the subject whole, from beginning to end in all its aspects."[12]

❖ *Are there parts of this assertion that you agree with?*

❖ *What do you disagree with?*

❖ *Do you have other comments you wish to make?*

Assertion 4: About History

All of us children of the twentieth century know, or should know, that there are no absolutes in human affairs, and thus there can be no such thing as perfect objectivity. We know that each historian in some degree creates the world anew and that all history is in some degree contemporary history.[13]

❖ *Are there parts of this assertion that you agree with?*

❖ *What do you disagree with?*

❖ *Do you have other comments you wish to make?*

Assertion 5: About Teaching and Learning History

Information provided by a teacher or textbook is generally, and wrongfully, perceived as knowledge. . . . Knowledge is something *created* through a process of personal involvement that allows for complex relationships between the learners (including the teacher) and the text and context of the classroom. . . . [emphasis in original][14]

❖ *Are there parts of this assertion that you agree with?*

❖ *What do you disagree with?*

❖ *Do you have other comments you wish to make?*

HERE I STAND: REDUCING AND CONSTRUCTING HISTORY

❖ *Do you enjoy history?*

❖ *Do you enjoy teaching history? What about it especially attracts or repels you?*

❖ *How would you describe the perspective from which* you *view the past? Is it centered in*

____ your personal background	____ ethnic group
____ culture	____ sexual orientation
____ politics	____ race
____ gender	____ disciplined objective study
____ nationality	____ . . . ?
____ religious faith	

❖ *Do you have an additional comment?*

❖ *Can you think of an example of how your perspective influences your teaching of history? What is your example?*

❖ *Do you agree that part of your task, and skill, as a history teacher is to "construct" — that is, organize, simplify, reduce, and present — history to your students? Why do you think that?*

❖ *When you think about history as something your students study, what is it you would like them to know?*

❖ *What do you think your students would say if you asked them to learn history largely from primary sources?*

❖ *What advantages and disadvantages do you see for you and your students if you relied on primary sources rather than a text (or textlike materials)?*

❖ *What issues you consider important were not raised in this chapter?*

❖ *How do you feel about these questions?*

NOTES

1. When teaching, I define primary sources broadly to include any documents, written materials, or artifacts that were created contemporaneous to the events they describe: for example, official documents; contemporary newspapers; diaries, journals, and letters; economic records; painting and sculpture; literature and poetry; and, more recently, photographs, movies, and videos.

2. See, for example, Louisa Schell Hoberman, "The Immigrant Experience and Student-Centered Learning: An Oral History Video Project," *Perspectives* 32, no. 3 (March 1994); Alice Lucas, ed., *Through Our Eyes: A Journal of Youth Writing*, (San Francisco: Zellerbach Family Fund, 1994); James A. Percoco, "History in the Making: The Development of a High School Applied History Program," *History News*, Sept.–Oct. 1994, pp. 8–12; Roy Rosenzweig, Steve Brier, and Josh Brown, *Who Built America?* CD-ROM, Voyager, 1993; *American Journey: Westward Expansion* CD-ROM, Primary Source Media, 1994; David Kobrin, Ed Abbot, John Ellinwood, and David Horton, "Learning History by Doing History," *Educational Leadership*, April 1993; *Concord Review*; teaching units available from the National Archives, e.g., "Westward Expansion: 1842–1912"; National Archives' document sets, e.g., "Internment of Japanese Americans"; *Teaching with Documents: Using Primary Sources from the National Archives* (Washington, DC: National Archives and National Council for the Social Studies, 1989); Cynthia Stokes Brown, *Connecting with the Past: History Workshop in Middle and High Schools* (Portsmouth, NH: Heinemann, 1994).

3. According to Gilbert Sewall, director of the American Textbook Council, 70 to 90 percent of history teaching today is "textbook driven and derived" (quoted in ASCD *Curriculum Update*, Winter 1995, p. 3).

4. Frances FitzGerald, *America Revisited: History Schoolbooks in the Twentieth Century* (Boston: Little, Brown, 1979), pp. 51–52.

5. See Herbert M. Kliebard and Barry M. Franklin, "The Course of the Course of Study: History Curriculum," in *Historical Inquiry in Education: A Research Agenda*, ed. John Hardin Best (Washington, D.C.: AERA, 1983), *passim*, and esp. p. 139; Suzanne M. Wilson, "Parades of Facts, Stories of the Past: What Do Novice History Teachers Need to Know," in *Teaching Academic Subjects to Diverse Learners*, ed. Mary M. Kennedy (New York: Teachers College Press, 1991), p. 112; FitzGerald, 1979, *passim*.

6. American Textbook Council, *History Textbooks: A Standard and Guide*, 1994, pp. 9–11; 13; 17–21.

7. John Anthony Scott, "*Lowen v. Turnispeed:* A Landmark Case," *American Historical Association Newsletter*, Oct., 1980.

8. *Education Week*, Oct. 24, 1990, p. 18.

9. For more on history and a constructivist perspective, see Russell H. Hvolbek, "History and Humanities: Teaching as Destructive of Certainty," in *History Anew: Innovations in the Teaching of History Today*, ed. Robert Blackey (Long Beach, CA: California State University Press, 1993), pp. 5–6; Robert F. Berkhofer, Jr., "Demystifying Historical Authority: Critical Textual Analysis in the Classroom," in *History Anew*, pp. 21–27; James A. Banks, "Social Science Knowledge and Citizenship Education," in *Teaching Academic Subjects to Diverse Learners*, ed. Mary M. Kennedy (New York: Teachers College Press, 1991), pp. 119, 121; James A. Banks, "Transforming the Mainstream Curriculum," *Educational Leadership* 51, no. 8 (May 1994):5–7; Jacqueline Grennon Brooks and Martin G. Brooks, *In Search of Understanding: The Case for Constructivist Classrooms* (Alexandria, VA: ASCD, 1993), pp. 23–30; *One Nation, Many Peoples: A Declaration of Cultural Interdependence*, The Report of the New York State Social Studies and Development Committee, 1991, p. ix. With regard to students creating history, see John Anthony Scott, "There Is Another Way: United States History Texts and the Search for Alternatives," *Perspectives*, May-June 1991; Donald H. Bragaw and H. Michael Hartoonian, "Social Studies: The Study of People in Society," in *Content of the Curriculum*, ed. Ronald S. Brandt (Alexandria, VA: ASCD, 1988), pp. 11; 27–28.

10. William H. Schubert, "Curriculum Reform," in *Challenges and Achievements of American Education*, ed. Gordon Cawelti (Alexandria, VA: ASCD, 1993), p. 92.

11. Philip Friedman, *Inadmissible Evidence* (New York: Donald I. Fine, 1992), p. 224 (a fictional dialogue about high school students at a drug rehabilitation center in NYC).

12. John A. Garraty, "Teaching and Textbooks," in *History Anew: Innovation in the Teaching of History Today*, ed. Robert Blackey, 1993, p. 107.

13. Frances FitzGerald, *America Revisited: History Schoolbooks in the Twentieth Century* (Boston: Little, Brown, 1979), p. 16.

14. Donald H. Bragaw and H. Michael Hartoonian, "Social Studies: The Study of People in Society," in *Content of the Curriculum*, ed. Ronald S. Brandt (Alexandria, VA: ASCD, 1988), p. 11.

2

For Their Own Reasons

WHAT A TEACHER CAN DO

For six years I worked collaboratively with teachers in the Providence, Rhode Island, public schools. Together we brainstormed ideas, planned units, and then cotaught a variety of history and social studies projects in their classrooms. All the projects asked students to use documents and other primary sources to study history, just as if the kids were themselves historians. This meant that they exercised unusual control, for students, over the history they studied, including the questions they wanted answered and the answers to those questions. Some of these projects used primary sources as the "text" to cover traditional content, like nineteenth-century America or Ancient Greece. Others used primary sources to explore complicated historical and methodological abstractions, such as what to do when internal evidence suggests that a source reveals more about the perspective of the writer than it does about its subject. Other units used primary sources for interdisciplinary work, which brought students from two schools together for discussions and peer evaluations of each other's writing.

The projects ranged from a yearlong experimental U.S. history class and a traditionally organized yearlong ninth-grade Western Civilization class to traveling two- and three-week units on various historical subjects that were repeated by four, and sometimes five, teachers in their own schools. We experimented in Advanced Placement U.S. history classes, in social studies electives like psychology and sociology, and in Western Civilization and U.S. history classes for students *designated by their schools* as mid- and lower-track.[1]

The public schools in which we worked varied considerably. One was an academic magnet school that required a written exam for admission. More than 90 percent of the students went to college after graduation. Daily attendance averaged well over 90 percent. In that school the students were perceived, by and large, as capable of doing challenging academic work. Students in college track classes were regularly asked to analyze, interpret, and weigh evidence, and then draw conclusions. Advanced Placement students worked with a variety of documents and other primary sources, including document-based questions from the AP exam.

The three other schools were dominated by students who, too often, were not seen by others, including in some cases those who taught them, as ready, willing, or able to face challenging academic tasks. For some adults, in and out of the school building, the dominant student "style" reinforced this perception. Despite the efforts of administrators and many teachers, the student culture in two of the schools generally held that leaving school in the middle of the day or being late for class or neglecting homework assignments was "normal" behavior hardly worthy of special notice. Once when I suggested to students who were working collaboratively that they might call one another at home, or find some other means of making contact outside of school if no phone was available, the idea was met with embarrassed laughter. That would be taking school too seriously.

Two of these schools also had highly transient student populations and in many classes actual daily absentee rates above twenty-five percent. A history class might have, say, twenty-eight students in the room in September and again in May, but a third or more of the students in May could be different from those who had been in the room in September. In one school the student population was so transient it was difficult for a consultant to determine the graduation rate: too many students moved in and out between ninth and twelfth grades to form a stable base from which percentages could be calculated.

Many of the young people in these schools came from economically disadvantaged families, some with annual family incomes below ten thousand dollars. A family might move within the city or to another city, and withdraw their children from class in the process, because of an adult's search for work. Sometimes a responsible student might stay home for several days to care for a younger sister or brother while his mother ran errands or worked. Or, a student might stay home to be with her own child despite daycare facilities in the school. Responsible students might not do homework because they worked twenty or more hours a week after school to help their family, or themselves.

The schools also had significant student populations of recent immigrants, some of whom were mainstreamed ESL students. The majority of these students' families had emigrated from various nations in Southeast Asia, Latin America, or the Caribbean islands. A bright and earnest ninth grader who I tutored told me excitedly one morning that his father had called from the Dominican Republic to say that he and his sister were to return home for a month. It would be great for him to see his father, whom I knew he missed (and for him to escape a New England winter). But how, I wondered, would he make up a month of classes? This student, like many of his peers, took a combination of bilingual and exclusively English language courses.

Our classroom experiences with the student historian approach were mixed. Over the years of our collaboration, however, we learned from our successes as well as our failures much about what was needed so that mainstreamed students in the schools could work successfully as student historians, constructing history from primary sources. One of the first lessons we learned is the crucial role of student motivation and involvement when working with primary sources. This was so no matter what the topic, which kids, or which school. To move away from what they were used to and toward working as student historians, the students needed to develop reasons of their own, which *they* found convincing. Unless they first went through a self-discovery process, when the time came to work as student historians they lacked the energy and intensity necessary to learn the skills and practice the self-discipline required. After all, no one can effectively analyze source materials, find patterns, and validate conclusions from the available records with a lackadaisical attitude.

How to involve students in school work is a question teachers must face, whatever the school or the subject. In more traditional classrooms, and those that follow what has been pejoratively termed the "banking" approach—the teacher's job is to open students' heads and deposit the valuables; later, tests check to see how much is left in the account—teacher energy and performance in front of the class are pivotal. But when it comes to student historian projects, the teacher's energy alone is never enough. It is the reasons students want to work that matter most. This is especially true for students who have known frustration and academic failure, including those for whom English, or the contemporary culture, is a second (or third) "language." For some, experience has taught that it can be painful to trust a teacher's word.

Since with the student historian approach it is the kids who must be involved actively, raising basic questions, defining answers, creating understandings, there are limits to what a teacher can say to motivate and involve the class. Prodding, threatening, goading, even sharing and modeling will not necessarily make students care about their work. They need to go through *a process* that will help them develop reasons of their own, even when that process is simply a longer route to the same answers their teacher could have given them. Most of the kids in our classes had no idea that studying history in school could involve deciding what questions are worth asking, what questions count because they make the past personally useful. Most did not understand that exercising choices in the classroom could help them find their own "voices."[2] It was as if they were constantly asking, Why do all this when it is easier to listen to the teacher?

When it came to getting kids to want to construct their own histories from documents and primary sources, we had to see and accept what we could and could not contribute. As teachers we were essential for the success of the class, no doubt about that. But our job was more one of helping the students understand the power inherent in the historian's work than of dominating the stage with our presence. As a team working together we could "model" our interest in the subject matter, willingness to take risks, patience with process, and tolerance for a variety of ideas. We could also frame and set up projects so that the history should seem "authentic" to the students. But, ultimately, it was the students who had to feel that this academic work mattered to them, that the classroom atmosphere we established and the learning we structured were valuable.

We learned not to leave it to chance. Instead, we developed a repertoire of classroom activities to help kids discover their own reasons for being involved with history. Beginning here was always necessary; otherwise, we could forget our hopes for effective student historian work, no matter what the students' past track records or the alleged "relevance" of the subject matter. When my colleagues and I were overconfident, or just plain tired, and thought this time we would skip the involvement activities—this was a "good" class, after all, that had done student historian work before—the consequences were always unpleasant and cumulative. Nothing that followed—collaborative group work, document analysis, written reports, oral presentations, or tests—was quite good enough. The measurable "outcomes" were better when we began with the question of how, on this topic, being a historian might touch the students personally.

Let me emphasize that we did not use our repertoire of involvement lessons for themselves. They were a setup, a necessary prelude to the serious work that followed. Students need considerable energy, self-discipline, and interest in order to read archaic primary sources carefully, take accurate notes, seek out patterns, draw conclusions, and write mini-histories in which they substantiate their statements with references to sources. The involvement exercises helped students develop reasons of their own for wanting to work hard on their history projects.

HERE I STAND: MOTIVATION AND INVOLVEMENT

❖ *Are there questions—private or public—that your study of history has helped you answer over the years? What would be an example?*

❖ *When it comes to involvement in school work, who has the primary responsibility, the teacher or the students?*
Is this an either/or question?

❖ *Picture in your mind some of the students in a favorite class. Knowing them as you do, why, exactly, do you think those kids should care about history as a subject of study?*

❖ *Picture in your mind some of the students in a class that was a problem for you. Why should those students care about history as a subject of study?*

❖ *If you shared these thoughts with actual students in your classes, do you think your ideas would make sense to them?*

FROM THE CLASSROOM

Few teachers I know voluntarily spend much time with theoretical models, no matter how steeped in authoritative research the theories are. It is not that teachers lack interest; to the contrary, teaching is their work. It is that so often seeing how to adapt the findings of educational research to practice is difficult. The chasm between theory and classroom is a real one. No matter which side of the divide you look from, you can see the gap.

I present "evidence" from actual classrooms because interesting ideas get us only so far until they are tried and tested by students and teachers in a classroom much like many others. Once ideas take on the richness of practice they become more easily usable food for thought. In this book, descriptions of classroom practice are the bridges offered to the reader's practice. (Classroom examples are included in this chapter, as well as Chapters 3, 4, and 5.) "Bridges," however, are different from "models." Teaching and learning history are too individualized a craft for templates to be a sufficient answer. A bridge, as metaphor, image, or illustration, is a way to connect our experimental work with someone else's, to connect teachers in one place with teachers in another. My hope is that the classroom examples offered in this book (with their high points and low points) will serve as prompts for further thinking. Their purpose is twofold: to offer nuanced examples of what student historian "theory" looks like when translated into classroom practice; and, more importantly, in doing so, to help you uncover approaches, methods and techniques that might work for you in your classroom.

The four examples in this chapter demonstrate activities and techniques we used specifically to help students find their own reasons to study history using primary sources. In order to focus on involvement, I have detached them from the unit as a whole. (Later chapters in this book discuss in some detail the student historian work that followed these involvement activities.)

These examples illustrate the developmental techniques for involving students that a more student-centered approach requires. When students are responsible participants helping to construct their own work, what is required of the teacher is less clear than in more traditionally taught classes because it *keeps changing* as students develop their understanding of history as a process, that is, how history is written, by whom, and, why it might matter to them. The teacher's involvement activities depend on where the class is at the time.

The first "From the Classroom" example, "Three Young Men of Color," introduced students in a traditional history class to two basic ideas: history is always written by someone; and "who controls the writing" of history is a power question they have reason to care about. Since over their school careers most students have probably encountered history largely in the form of facts and ideas (including debates among historians) to be learned and memorized, provoking interest in how historians work and in the possibility of working as historians themselves was a necessary first step in their development as student historians. Otherwise, why should they take primary sources more seriously than, say, the textbook?

Once students had at least an initial understanding of the constructivist approach to history, they were ready to struggle with "construction" problems themselves. The second classroom example, "Hermaphrodites as Laborers," shows how ninth graders who tackled primary sources ripe with methodological complications got seriously involved in questions about how to write accurate history. The analysis and synthesis problems they encountered became captivating puzzles they needed to resolve. Their sense of why they might want to work as student historians—their involvement with history—was strengthened and broadened by the experience of working with challenging primary sources.

The third example, "The United States Fights Wars," describes techniques used to help all the students in a class discover individual reasons for studying the United States' involvement in wars from 1812 to 1991. In our experience, the hope that students would accept the teacher's interest as valid for themselves was never enough to make a class work well. To care about a historical topic, they had to uncover personal connections that made sense to each of them.

The classroom activities in the final example, "Civil Rights, 1919–1960s," were designed for students who were involved with the topic but not necessarily with history. This is especially important in studying "relevant" and highly charged historical issues like racism and prejudice. Enthusiasm for the subject matter does not automatically mean that students are learning about the past. They need to be involved with the past as well as with themselves. Here, once again, the classroom teacher plays a crucial role.

THREE YOUNG MEN OF COLOR

Involvement activities were usually keyed to the historical content of the upcoming unit. Out of necessity, however, we also developed a generic one-day lesson that raised questions about where "history" comes from. We wanted students to ask themselves: Could there be more to history than understanding the textbook narrative? What is gained, and lost, by dealing with primary sources? Should we "create" history in our classroom if our teacher helps us?

Our method was to tell the class a pointed, fictional story about the role of the written record in people's lives. The moral of the story, bluntly stated, is that whoever controls the account of what happened in the past defines history. The story, as retold here, is appropriate for high school. To be equally effective with younger students, details in the story line would have to be adjusted to fit better the life experiences of those students. Seventh or eighth graders, for instance, are less likely than eleventh or twelfth graders to be working the night shift at a fast-food restaurant. But, needless to say, many have intense feelings about relationships and identity, the key elements in the narrative.

The story was about three young men of color (from whichever school we were in) who were arrested while walking late at night on a local street near their school, apparently for no other reason than responding to racial harassment from white police officers. Even subtle changes in how the story was told, its tone and pacing, and the extent to which students participated in creating the story, affected what they learned.

The story starts with one of the young men in particularly bad spirits because his girlfriend broke up with him that morning. Not only that, she also used the occasion to pour out bile she said she had always felt. That was news to the young man, who had no sense of how bad things were. When his friends meet him later, around eleven-thirty, after his night shift at the Burger King, he is in no mood to accept harassment from anyone. So when the white police officers who stop the young men make a racial comment without anything the young men think is provocation, the student responds in kind. The result is bruises, a night spent in the police station, and very worried mothers for at least two of the young men.

Telling the story usually created considerable tension in the room. Whether the class was predominantly black, Asian, and Latino or mostly white, the story touched students' anger and fear, but this is what produced the opportunity for learning. However, having unleashed strong feelings, we needed to safeguard the students in the room. The discussion that followed dealt first with personal experiences and feelings, and only later drew conclusions. We needed a controlled way to express and defuse emotions before facing the issues as a class.

Most of the students in the classroom shared the same perspective as the fictional students: they believed the three young men had been unfairly arrested. The kids felt sure that once the news of the students' arrest and night in jail got around the school, almost everyone their age would believe they had been treated unfairly. The teacher telling the story pointed out that because the police officers exercised the power of the historian in writing out the official case report, their perspective prevailed. As a result, no matter whose account was more accurate, the three friends spent the night in jail. Anyone who checked that day's local newspaper or the police blotter five years from now, the teacher added, would probably learn only the police officers' version of what had happened.

Were the students in this class willing, the teacher asked while holding up their U.S. history textbook, to have the perspectives of the authors of their text tell them who *their* people were? Or would they grab that power for themselves—would they be historians—if we helped them do it?

- ❖ *The "Three Young Men" story was usually effective in persuading high school students to give the student historian approach a try. Why do you think that was so?*

- ❖ *The "Three Young Men" story is "political" in the sense that a) it has a clear point of view; b) it suggests certain conclusions; and c) it implies definite values. Is it too "slanted" for your taste as a history teacher? In what ways?*

- ❖ *Could you change the story so it becomes a classroom teaching tool you would use?*

- ❖ *Is it possible to involve students in creating history without raising political and values questions?*

- ❖ *Is it possible for a teacher to study history without raising these same political and values questions?*

HERMAPHRODITES AS LABORERS

The "Three Young Men of Color" story raises questions about the accuracy of historical accounts. If honest observers can disagree about the same event, how can historians know years later, sometimes hundreds or thousands of years later, what actually happened? When students think about it, just the idea that history is "constructed" rather than retold can be disquieting. This is especially true for middle and high school age students. With so much of their lives already in flux, they have a lower tolerance for ambiguity. When something seems amiss, they often have energy—instantly—for the necessary repair work. When students face the methodological complications of learning history from primary sources directly, they can become involved for reasons that seem genuine to them. Successfully "constructing" a "history" through primary sources can feel to adolescents like putting their world back in order.

The classroom teacher and I both felt some dissonance while planning the "The Age of Discovery" unit for his ninth-grade Western Civilization class. The subject seemed to us a prime example of how ethnocentrism can influence an apparently objective perspective. To say "new" worlds were "discovered" is to learn about indigenous people from a European perspective. Furthermore, most, but not all, extant primary sources on North American peoples in the sixteenth and seventeenth centuries are European in origin. Whose viewpoint on "The Age of Discovery" should we adopt, and why? Perhaps we could structure a limited concrete case and let the students (try to) decide.

The ninth graders in this Western Civilization class had just finished studying the Renaissance, so they had some information about Europeans exploring what to them were strange lands. We provided minimal additional background and then passed out photocopies of a sixteenth-century drawing, made by a European, of muscular Native Americans in what is now the southeastern United States carrying sick people on stretchers or piggyback. The drawing, which included a written description, was titled "Hermaphrodites as Laborers" (see Figure 2–1). We began, as we often did, by going over the primary source together as a class. It took a good ten minutes of studying the drawing, reading the brief description below the picture aloud, checking vocabulary words, and answering students' questions before, finally, a ninth grader asked, "What does 'hermaphrodite' mean?"

Trying to sound as if it was just another word the ninth graders did not know, I defined *hermaphrodite* as a plant or animal that has the sexual characteristics of both males and females. The stunned silence was followed shortly by a flurry of predictable questions and renewed scrutiny of the pic-

HERMAPHRODITES AS LABORERS

Hermaphrodites are common in these parts. They are considered odious, but are used as beasts of burden, since they are strong. Whenever the Indians go to war, it is the hermaphrodites who carry the provisions. And whenever an Indian dies, be it from wounds or from disease, it is the hermaphrodites who carry the dead to the burial ground. They lay the deceased on a woven mat of reeds attached to crosspieces on stout poles. One skin is placed under the head, a second about the body, a third around one thigh, a fourth around one leg. Why this is done I never discovered, but I suppose it is for ornamentation, since sometimes they bind a skin around only one leg. Then the hermaphrodites take thongs of hide, fasten them to the ends of the poles, and rest these upon their heads (which are remarkably hard), and in this way they carry the bodies to the burial ground.

The hermaphrodites also look after those who have contagious diseases; they take the sick on their shoulders to places selected for the purpose and feed and care for them until they are well again.

FIG. 2–1: *Hermaphrodites as Laborers*

ture. Only then were students ready to accept that the European author of the primary source was saying the human beings he had observed *were* hermaphrodites. Cognitive dissonance reigned supreme for the remainder of the period!

Students searched aloud for ways to reconcile the drawing and its accompanying text with their own knowledge of the world. Among their tentative hypotheses: the painter must have meant the plants not the people; they, the students, were stupid and could not understand; it was a joke; and, finally, just before the bell, what the source really showed was muscular men who crossed gender expectations by compassionately caring for the sick. The kids had begun to consider whether all sources are reliable.

The next day we added five more pictorial primary sources created by Europeans who visited North America in the sixteenth century.[3] Each included a brief written description. We selected them because their accuracy could be questioned using the internal evidence of the source itself, and because thoughtful consideration could produce inferences about the authors of the material, a concept that proved difficult for many students in the class to grasp. One source, for instance, showed natives collecting silver and brass in Appalachian Mountain streams. Another, which rivaled the hermaphrodite source in inspiring student disbelief, pictured natives creeping up to unsuspecting live deer by disguising themselves in deer carcasses (see Figure 2–2).

HUNTING DEER

The Indians hunt deer in a way we have never seen before. They hide themselves in the skin of a very large deer which they have killed some time before. They place the animal's head upon their own head, looking through the eye holes as through a mask. In this disguise they approach the deer without frightening them. They choose the time when the animals come to drink at the river, shooting them easily with bow and arrow.

To protect their left forearm from the bowstring, they usually wear a strip of bark. And they prepare the deerskins without any iron instruments, using only shells, in a surprisingly expert way. I do not believe any European could do this better.

FIG. 2–2: Hunting Deer

Is it possible that humans with arms and legs sticking out of animal skins could get that close to live deer? one student wanted to know. Wouldn't their smell give them away? Maybe deer back then were different, another student suggested. A third thought maybe the guy from Europe was adding drama to a hunting method he had seen so he could sell more books in Europe. Most kids agreed that there was no way to know for sure from the sources.

Throughout the one-week unit the ninth graders generally worked intensely. Organized in small groups (a classroom method that raises interesting questions of its own I will return to in Chapter 3) and using worksheets we designed for the project (see Figure 2–3), the students painstakingly described what they thought the primary sources revealed about the people who lived in North America in the 1500s, and what they might infer from the sources about the European authors of those sources. (The worksheets asked them to include exactly how each source led them to their conclusions.) The ninth graders remained involved because they found the methodological puzzles we had set for them intriguing and challenging, but not too frustrating.

❖ *Can you think of readily available primary sources that might present intriguing methodological puzzles to your students? What would be an example?*

❖ *What problems would you anticipate if you used such an approach with one of your classes?*

❖ *Can you think of "solutions" for at least some of these teaching problems?*

❖ *Do you think such an approach would involve your students in their work? How so?*

THE UNITED STATES FIGHTS WARS: FROM THE WAR OF 1812 THROUGH THE GULF WAR OF 1991

To most history teachers it is obvious that a knowledge of the past is a valuable asset, and one worth working for. Because this seems so clear to them, some teachers make the mistake of assuming that, with a little explanation, the value of learning history will be equally clear to everyone in their classroom.

Telling kids how much they would benefit from knowing about the past, however, is as likely to backfire as succeed. Pearls of wisdom are not

FIG. 2–3: Students as Historians—The Age of Discovery

Your name: _____

Number and name of visual primary source: # _____

1. Describe <u>in your own words</u> what this visual primary source tells you about the people who lived in North America in the fifteen hundreds. (Be sure to include <u>how you know that</u> by telling what exactly in the source led you and your partners to your conclusions.)

2. Describe in your own words what the visual primary source tells you about the people who came from Europe to North America in the fifteen hundreds. (Be sure to include <u>how you know that</u> by telling what exactly in the source led you and your partners to your conclusions.)

always appreciated just because they drop from a teacher's mouth. Instead, it is the ideas students "self-discover," with a teacher's guidance and structure, that are more likely to carry genuine meaning and produce authentic student involvement.

When we introduced "The United States Fights Wars" unit in U.S. history classes, we started with personal questions rather than the usual background information. This allowed us to stress two important points: that all historians write from a values perspective and that students' values strongly influence how they understand, evaluate, and use or ignore the history that they study in school. In making these points we found that our examples, words, and phrases needed to be fine-tuned to the developmental level, experience, and sensitivities of the students in the room.

These introductory activities were intended not as "values clarification" exercises, although they might seem to be, but rather as ways of involving students, of helping them discover reasons that made sense to them why studying one hundred and eighty years of war could be personally important.

We began by asking the kids to find paper, or use their journals if they had them, for a private "writing for thinking" exercise. In the silence of a serious classroom, we asked them to write about the two things they valued most in life at that moment. Then we asked them to add what they valued most about themselves as individuals, an assignment that was difficult for some of them. We asked no questions after they finished, but if they wanted to read what they had written aloud, we paused for brief statements.

As a transition and introduction to the next activity we distinguished between being willing to kill to achieve a goal or protect a value on the one hand, and being willing to give your life to achieve a goal or protect a value on the other. We then moved the chairs to create a plazalike open space in the middle of the classroom. With kids, and teachers when they were willing or thought it wise, standing bunched in the "plaza," we literally walked ourselves through a series of choices that would be telling for these students. Decide between fast cars and being loved. If you would rather have fast cars, walk toward the windows; if being loved is your first choice, move toward the wall. And if you are not sure, just stay where you are. Or, how about deciding between good food and good friends, or having a TV and having a family? We used the same public walking technique for statements about what you would die for or kill for, the distinction raised in the transition discussion: Your country, right or wrong? To protect someone you love? To keep your self-respect? Fast cars and good shopping?

Next we turned to how history can be used to answer current questions. For instance, when the next war comes, the president of the United States is likely to marshal arguments about why you, when you are old enough, should put your life on the line. If past experience is any guide, some of these inducements will include historical precedents and interpreted events offered as fact. Would a president purposely mislead you on such an important matter? we asked the class. How could you find out? Have presidents in the past always been honest with their constituents on matters of "national security"? Does it matter? That is, not is it morally "right" or "wrong," but could your life, or the lives of those you love, depend on it?

When these two days of introductory exercises and discussions worked well, the students were primed to confront the United States at war, through a set of documents and primary materials, from a personal perspective. When the involvement activities did not go so well, school being school, we soldiered on anyway.

❖ *Do these involvement activities seem too much like "values clarification" exercises to deserve a place in your history classroom?*

❖ *Do you agree, as I contend in this example, that students need to discover their own reasons for studying history, even if those reasons wind up being conclusions you could have told them at the start?*

CIVIL RIGHTS, 1919–1960s

Even with "naturally" involving historical topics like racism and the civil rights movement, we discovered that it was a mistake to assume we could skip involvement activities. Common sense might suggest that relevant history subjects would hold student interest, but in reality, there are too many variables for the matter to be that straightforward. Sometimes high interest can change to boredom when the work gets under way. We are talking, after all, about studying the past with energy and self-discipline using documents and primary sources, not about students trading opinions based on the story of their lives. There is a difference between students' excitement about issues that are currently relevant to them and their continuing involvement in a serious, organized study of history.

The unit on the civil rights movement in the United States, from 1919 through the mid-1960s, was taught concurrently in two classes, an Advanced Placement U.S. history class and a psychology elective, in two quite different high schools. I began by asking students to picture their upcoming junior or senior prom—friends, decorations, strobe lights, and all. As they scanned the dance hall in their minds, I asked them to record in private writing for themselves their first reactions when they saw an Asian woman from their school, whom they knew, dancing with an African American man they did not recognize; then, their reactions when they spotted two guys, dressed to the hilt, dancing together; and, finally, their reactions when they saw two women, both in low-cut gowns, also apparently prom dates. Were the students surprised by their own reactions? We hoped they were. The exercise was intended to help students raise to consciousness issues they might previously have kept tucked away.

That wake-up call was followed by a discussion about methodology. On the chalkboard I wrote the essential question for our discussion: "How do you know what you know?" I asked the students who in their school faced the most prejudice. Both classes, psychology and A.P. history, agreed on gays and lesbians first, followed by Asians. The "factual" issue resolved, I then asked, "How do you know that?" Shared incidents from lunchrooms and locker rooms and a class consensus on their prevalence left the students feeling confident they had the right answer. But when we switched our attention to the city as a whole the question was less easily answered, and the response was the same in both classes. According to the kids, again arguing from their own experience, the pattern was too changeable from neighborhood to neighborhood to say that one group rather than another faced the most prejudice in the city. Certain Asian American students, for instance, reported that they felt safe in one part of the city but would not think of walking alone in other neighborhoods, an experience that resonated with the experiences of many other kids in the room. Finally, when we tried the same question for the entire United States, it was immediately obvious to most students why we could not answer it without more information. And that insight was, of course, the principal objective behind the discussion. If the students were interested in studying racism, discrimination, and civil rights, sharing what they already knew would not be enough.

The following class day, hunting for precision and some shared understanding, we turned to the meaning of commonly used words. *Discrimination, prejudice, stereotype, racism*, all are words bandied about in everyday speech. But is the meaning of each, I asked, always the same for everyone? What about people, for instance, who are not blatant racists but consistently choose to live in segregated neighborhoods and send their children to *de facto* segregated schools? Are they passive contributors to racism? Should such "choices" be considered racist behavior? Furthermore, could the very idea of the existence of races, itself a cultural construct, be seen as racist, as Ashley Montagu has suggested.[4] We talk, after all, about "blacks" and "whites," never about "tallies" and "shorties." Everyone knows, to follow this absurd analogy, that shorties cannot do college-level work. Nothing against them. That's just the way it is.

Only after these introductory involvement activities and discussions did we turn to the next task, asking students to choose questions they wanted to answer about the history of the civil rights movement in the United States. Primed to care (we hoped!) about how they could learn more and why they might want to, armed with documentary sources and worksheets, the students were ready to begin the real work of the unit: studying history through source materials.

❖ *Do you agree that relevant subject matter by itself will not always involve students in their study of history?*

❖ *In your experience, has initial high interest in a history subject turned to boredom—even resentment—once the hard work started? Do you have an example?*

❖ *Do you think it overstates the case to say that teacher "energy" can backfire when it comes to involving students in their work?*

❖ *Are involvement activities (like those described in this chapter) worth the class time that they take? Why?*

❖ *What issues that you think are important were not raised in this chapter?*

NOTES

1. These collaborations included teaching with Ed Abbott, Jim Charleson, the late Nick Christopher, John Ellinwood, Chris Hayes, David Horton, Albin Moser, Brenda Rudman, and Peter Waddington.

2. John Duffy, presentation at the AHA annual conference, Dec. 28, 1992.

3. All are reprinted in Stefan Lorant, ed., *The New World* (New York: Duell, Sloan, and Pearce, 1946).

4. Ashley Montagu, *Statement on Race* (New York: Schuman, 1951).

3

Setting the Table

STUDENTS TEACHING STUDENTS

Experimenting with student historian projects in city schools I often felt like an explorer from days gone by. I wished I could send the scouts around the next bend to find out what lay ahead. Like my colleagues, I tried to project a teacherly kind of self-assurance the kids could depend on. In fact, I was often surprised by major developments I had not anticipated. Some of those surprises felt almost like ambushes and left us wounded and pondering retreat. But the unanticipated could also be good news.

Our experience taught us, for instance, that students must depend on one another. When history classes move away from the "banking" model to a more student-centered "discovery" approach, the job of student historian—initiating questions, analyzing documents, creating and validating interpretations—is too demanding for most middle and high school kids to do alone. The truth of the matter is that, faced directly, problems of historical interpretation and field definition can be overwhelming for adolescents and young adults. Too often they are used to receiving "solid" answers.

With few exceptions, mainstreamed students in the schools where we taught were capable of working as student historians, that is, actually constructing the history they studied from primary sources, but success required a specific approach. For projects to succeed, students had to teach other students. What made it possible for mainstreamed students to learn history through primary sources was that students with diverse life experiences and perspectives, and varied learning styles, worked together in a group. The same characteristics sometimes labeled learning problems in more traditionally organized classes became essential assets when kids cooperated. Complex analytic tasks that might be too much for one student working alone could be tackled more easily when several students contributed what they knew, what they felt, and how they thought. Gender differences, racial perspectives, first languages other than English, recent immigrant and native-born experiences, even social and economic class gaps all became tools the kids could use to unravel the complicated human stories hidden in documents and primary sources—as long as they willingly depended on one another.

And that was the rub. To do student historian projects we needed classrooms where cooperative habits and attitudes were the pervasive norm. Yet the dominant culture for many of our students, in and out of school, was a highly assertive, almost anti-intellectual individualism. "Normal" everyday behavior included strident and loud public banter; in many schools, the kids regularly used harsh, derogatory words against one another. It seemed a far cry from there to the collaborative attitudes the students would need to succeed as historians.

What were we to do? Changing students' attitudes about the value of learning from other students as well as from their teacher is a complicated task. It is especially difficult with kids who expect to sit in rows, listen to presentations, or work alone from a book. Teachers who have tried cooperative methods or attended collaborative workshops know that you cannot just push chairs together, pass out an assignment, and say, "Go to it!"[1] Should we expect to spend weeks, or longer, on cooperative skill-building exercises, in addition to the absolutely necessary involvement exercises, *before* we engaged students in serious work with primary sources?

When we did see around the next "bend," however, we were surprised to discover that in tackling student historian projects the kids consistently took to collaborative tasks and worked together easily and effectively, that is, in comparison to the general work habits in the school at large. It was enthralling to watch. Across varied projects and in more than one school, the kids developed the classroom culture we teachers longed for without our being fully aware at the time of how it happened. Time and again they seemed to take "naturally" to helping one another. They read difficult primary sources aloud, deciphered archaic phrases or puzzling pictures, discussed, analyzed and reanalyzed, and eventually even reached consensus on their conclusions. In classes that included mainstreamed ESL students, recent immigrants, and native-born students whose first language was not English, group members helped one another over writing and reading comprehension hurdles. With worksheets that outlined limited tasks, kids peer edited one another's essays. They initiated and then divided among themselves (and most often carried out) tasks they wanted done, like coloring maps or photocopying pictures. Organized into groups, they successfully taught—they did not just present, they taught—the remainder of the class what they, on their own, had studied. Discussions sometimes sounded more like colleagues exchanging ideas than kids cutting each other down to size. And when all was said and done, test scores, both on content-centered, objective-type tests and less traditional final projects, were at least as good as when the same class learned similar material using more individually oriented methods.

We can celebrate the students' real achievements as collaborators without denying that the going could be difficult, or that progress could be slow and erratic. In some classes students at first refused to work with individuals from a different race or ethnic background. Others crossed off classmates based on personality conflicts or gender. Patience and strict adherence to a rule requiring everyone to state their beliefs in a way that respected those of all others—try to imagine how someone else might hear your words, we said—were helpful. Anger and moral outrage were not. We also contended with high schoolwide absentee rates, sometimes more than a quarter of all students, which played havoc with day-to-day consistency in groups. We resisted group members' requests to take their work home, relying instead on folders that we filed in the classroom. Otherwise the next day some of the group and all the work might be missing.

HERE I STAND: STUDENTS TEACHING STUDENTS

❖ *How regularly do you use collaborative methods for teaching history (if at all)?*

❖ *If you use collaborative activities, which of these problems have you encountered?*

    ____ The academically stronger do the lion's share of the work.

    ____ It is hard to devise a grading system that evaluates kids individually when they are working as a group.

    ____ Classroom management and discipline are difficult: you can't be in two, or three, or four places simultaneously.

    ____ Cooperative projects take so much time it's hard to cover the mandated curriculum.

❖ *What strategies have you devised to help you deal with the problems you have encountered?*

❖ *In your experience, what are the most important benefits, for students and teachers, of working collaboratively (rather than individually)?*

TEACHERS SET THE TABLE

Why student historians were able to collaborate so well was a puzzle at the time. Now it seems obvious, and wonderful. Birds flocking—in a park, in the wild, from a lawn—provide a graphic analogy. Recent computer-based research in biology shows that birds strange to one another can fly in perfect formations. How did they learn their synchronized flights, suddenly swooping gracefully or fluidly changing directions? They look as if they had practiced forever under the guidance of an expert and demanding teacher. In fact, however, they are acting as autonomous organisms, each bird following a set of simple rules that satisfy its own private needs. Each bird is centered in its immediate, personal environment, yet the result is a complex group collaboration.

It is common for individuals, even people who might not trust each other or care much about one another, to cooperate in groups. Kids who might be hostile in some situations, for example, can be highly attuned to the group in other situations. Imagine students planning a school dance, or a weekend party, or an African American heritage club meeting, or a car wash to raise money for Close-Up, or a ski trip. Whatever the example, when the group works well, the kids usually divide the jobs themselves, relying on their personal styles and needs to decide who should do what. Those who love to talk might volunteer to make the phone calls; a student who cannot stand "messes" might create a "things-to-do" list and then cross off jobs completed; physically active kids might be happiest getting supplies or moving furniture; a student with a car might want to provide transportation; those who love drawing might make posters. The result is the "natural" creation of a working collaboration.

As teachers, we had been trying to solve the wrong problem. It was not so much that students' attitudes needed changing. They could, when they wanted to, suddenly access the required cooperative attitudes, as if on demand. The principal problem was getting the incentives for cooperation right. Why should they want to collaborate in the history classroom? The key in and out of classrooms is that students must believe cooperation is in their own self-interest. Then, like birds flocking, individuals are capable of surprisingly complex collaborative endeavors. As we discovered, when the right incentives came together, students collaborated because they wanted to. Which brings up a new question: How do you get students to understand that cooperating on the work their teacher requires is in their own self-interest?

That question, which may sound as if it requires magic, emphasizes the crucial role of the teacher. To say that the kids cooperated student-to-student "because they wanted to," and only when they wanted to, could make it seem that responsibility rested solely with them. Not so. The students' desire to collaborate as historians depended on the careful structure we teachers gave their classroom experience.

As strange as the analogy may sound, teachers and chefs have much in common. When I worked as a cook in restaurants I was taught that people eat with their eyes as well as their mouths. The cooks in the kitchen, and the waiters and waitresses on the floor staff, paid attention to how food was set on the plate and how the plate was set on the table. That the food was nutritious, delicious, and finely prepared, and the customers hungry, was crucial. But it was never sufficient.

In working as teachers with student historians, our job was analogous but more complicated. It involved setting a table that appealed to appetites students might not even know they had, like the urge to use school work to grow and mature as individuals. The students needed our guidance, organization, and support. To "set the table" meant creating the classroom conditions that prompted students to cooperate with one another "naturally" on history projects.

To the extent that we were able to satisfy the following conditions, virtually all the students worked together because they wanted to:

We designed involvement activities for each project to help students see that they could have some of the personal power of being a historian in their own hands and find good reasons of their own to care about the history topic under study.

And we structured the projects so that it was obvious they needed one another to complete them. We had two avenues of recourse here: how students were to do their work and how they were graded. (The role and function of grades will be discussed more fully in Chapter 5.)

FROM THE CLASSROOM: THE RENAISSANCE

To illustrate "table setting" I have chosen a unit on the Renaissance, which the classroom teacher and I taught to his ninth-grade Western Civilization class, because it shows what we did in practice to encourage cooperation. More specifically, we

- designed and carried out involvement activities
- created written structures that subdivided tasks and clarified for students what we expected of them
- organized students' work so that it was difficult for anyone to complete the unit without depending on others
- used a grading and evaluation system that rewarded students who turned to other students to learn
- modeled our own collaboration in the classroom every day.

The historical content of the Renaissance unit was much like what might be found in a traditional textbook or set of textbooks for middle or high school students. The difference was that we were asking students to learn history by analyzing primary sources in collaborative groups and then teach each other the historical content they alone had studied. The primary sources the class used were readily available—some, in fact, were reprinted in their textbook—and included pictures of Benvenuto Cellini's *Perseus*, Michelangelo's *Pietà*, and Verrocchio's *Lorenzo de' Medici*; a fourteenth-century map; an excerpt from Machiavelli's *The Prince*; one of Petrarch's sonnets; and an excerpt from Pico della Mirandola's "Oration on the Dignity of Man." We also provided references to pages in the students' text where they could find background information on the sources.

We began the Renaissance unit with what seemed to us to be the most important initial question: Why should anyone in the room care about the Renaissance? Earlier in the year the ninth graders had heard and discussed the emotionally powerful fictional story of the "Three Young Men of Color."[2] This class had been so captivated by the original telling that several days later they wanted a follow-up story with a different ending: "Three Young Men of Color, Part II." Yet when we resuscitated the story for what we thought would be a quick review, what had been a live topic now evoked minimal response. Well, we thought, the earth in our garden needs turning again. We opted for an impromptu discussion to help kids remember what it means to work as student historians.

To awaken interest in the Renaissance itself we introduced the period as a time when, despite the more than four-century time difference, people seemed uncannily like us. Take love, for example. People in the Renaissance, we said, could tell us something about our own feelings. We began with rhetorical questions: Can love hurt? Are there gender differences in the way people love? Is "adult" love different from "adolescent" love? Is being in love always the same as acting on it? Adolescents can respond with considerable vigor to rhetorical questions.

Next, we gave each student a copy of Petrarch's sonnet, "I Find No Peace, Yet Am Not Armed for War" (Figure 3–1), and a copy of our own creation, a "Historian's Worksheet for Detecting Information on the Renaissance" (versions of this worksheet are shown in Figures 3–4 and 3–5). If we assume, we said to the class, that Petrarch's poem is an accurate reflection of the views of people during the Renaissance—if, just for this class, we act as if this one sonnet is a universe of accurate information—then what conclusions can we draw from it about views on love during the Renaissance? After reading the poem aloud, we asked students, working with a partner, to write on their worksheet "Adjectives, Information, Conclusions" that described what people in the Renaissance thought about "love." In the rather free-wheeling discussion that followed, the students compared ideas about love, and the teachers made sure to ask, How do you know that? What in

FIG. 3–1: Petrarch's Sonnet

I Find No Peace, Yet Am Not Armed for War

I find no peace, yet am not armed for war
In Hope I fear, in ice I burn and gasp;
I lie on earth, and in the sky I soar,
Embrace the universe, and nothing clasp.

She holds me trapped with neither lock nor noose,
Nor keeps me for her own, nor breaks the chain;
And Love itself will neither slay nor loose,
Nor let me live, nor free me from my pain.

I have no eyes, yet see; no tongue, yet cry,
I long to perish, yet I voice my fears;
Myself I hate, and for another sigh,
I joy in sorrow, and I smile in tears;
For death and life alike I am unfit,
And you, my lady, are the cause of it.

---

the poem—our universe of accurate information—leads you as a historian to your conclusion?

We hoped that these activities would "prompt" students to discover why they might want to study the Renaissance through primary sources. In addition, the involvement activities introduced students to the basic project format. Students were divided into six collaborative groups of about four students each. Each group member was given a set of three or four primary sources, and a "Historian's Worksheet for Detecting Information on the Renaissance" keyed to those particular sources. No two groups shared the same sources. Every collaborative group's first task was to go through the same process with their primary sources that the class as a whole had modeled using Petrarch's love sonnet: "Assuming that your sources are an accurate 'universe' of information," we repeated, "what conclusions can you, as a group, draw from them about the Renaissance? Write that information on your worksheet."

We had set up the required work for the unit so that individual success depended on cooperation. The worksheets served as a written "structure," or guide, to encourage and require collaboration. All the students filled out an individual worksheet listing the conclusions they had drawn from their sources, and these worksheets were collected and graded. But it was the "Clerk's" completed worksheet—a consensus product of the group as a

FIG. 3-2: Machiavelli, excerpt from The Prince

It is a good thing for a prince to be considered generous. But if generosity is concealed, no one will ever hear about it. Unless he advertises his generosity, the prince will become known as a miser. To earn a reputation as a generous prince, therefore, many men finance lavish displays and put on costly shows. But if a prince does this, he will spend most of his money on displays. If he is to continue to appear generous, he will have to impose heavy taxes and do everything possible to obtain more funds. This course of action will make his subjects begin to hate him; they will not even respect him because he will be poor. His generosity will have injured many and benefited only a few....For these reasons a prince must not worry if he becomes known as a miser....

Is it better for a prince to be loved more than feared? Or is it better to be feared more than loved? Ideally, a prince ought to be both feared and loved, but it is difficult for subjects to hold both sentiments toward their ruler. If one of the two must be sacrificed, it is much safer for a prince to be feared rather than loved. In general, men are ungrateful, dishonest, cowardly, and covetous. As long as you help them, they will do what you want them to do. They will offer you their blood, their goods, their lives, and their children when it appears that you will not need to take them up on their word. If a prince has relied solely on the good faith of others, he will be ruined. Men are less afraid to offend a prince they love than one they fear....

I conclude, therefore, that men have control of their love for a prince, but the prince, himself, controls their fear of him. The wise prince will rely on what he can control and not what others control. He must be careful, however, not to make men hate him.

Everyone knows that it is a good thing for a prince to keep his word and live a faithful life. The history of our own times shows, however, that those princes who have done great things have not worried about keeping their word. A successful prince must imitate both the lion and the fox. In imitating the lion, the prince protects himself from wolves. In imitating the fox, he protects himself from traps....A prince ought not to keep his word if doing so would go against his best interests....If all men were good, this rule would not be a sound one. But because they are bad, and do not honor their word to the prince, he is not bound to keep his word....

It is not necessary for a prince to have all the good qualities that I have named, but it is necessary that he seem to have them. I will even go so far as to say that to actually have these qualities and to be guided by them always is dangerous. But to appear to have them is useful. It is well, therefore, to seem merciful, faithful, sincere, religious, and also to be so. But a prince must be always ready to have the opposite qualities if need be. New princes, particularly, fail when they have these good qualities. In order to maintain their power they often must act against faith, against charity, against humanity and against religion. A prince must be ready to shift with the wind as the ups and downs of fortune require. He should not go against what is good if he can avoid it, but he should be ready and able to do evil when necessary.

I conclude, then, that if fortune continues to vary and men remain basically the same, princes will be successful so long as their ways fit the circumstances. But when times call for other tactics, they will fail unless they follow a new course. I certainly think it is better to act impetuously than to act cautiously, for fortune is a woman, and if the prince wishes to master her, he must conquer her by force. She is overcome by the bold rather than by those who proceed coldly. And, therefore, like a woman, she is always a friend to the young because they are less cautious, more fierce, and master her with greater audacity [daring].

FIG. 3–3: Verrocchio's Bust of Lorenzo de' Medici

whole—that served as the "checkpoint" for everyone in the group. The group could not advance to the second part of their work, their oral presentations, without completing individual worksheets *and* the consensus worksheet, which required approval indicated by a teacher's initials at the bottom of the page. When students and teachers adhered strictly to the collaborative structure, either the group advanced together or no one moved forward. It was in every student's self-interest to make sure that everyone else was keeping up—assuming involvement and a desire to complete the project.

The "Historian's Worksheet" directed the group members to divide other administrative responsibilities among themselves so that they took turns being in charge. (Roving the room, the teachers checked that each group followed through.) The "President's" efforts to facilitate discussions and group writing could be ignored by others, of course. Yet students usually came to understand fairly rapidly that given their varied backgrounds, learning styles and interrelated strengths and weaknesses, they would do better as student

FIG. 3–4: Historian's Worksheet for Detecting Information on the Renaissance

Your name:_____

Before you begin, you must choose roles for your group work. One of you will be the <u>President</u>. The job of the President is to make sure that everyone in the group helps out and that the group gets its work done on time. The job of the <u>Clerk</u> is to keep an accurate set of notes. (Everyone is also to fill in completely her or his own worksheet.) The job of the <u>Presenter</u> is to lead the group's presentation when teaching the rest of the class what you learned from your documents.

The President is_____   The Clerk is_____

The Presenter is_____

<u>Group 1</u>: Petrarch. Humanism
Gaspara Stampa. Woman poet of the Renaissance
(You must use both documents. For background
information, see in your text pp. 356–358.)

Adjectives, Info., Conclusions	Where you found it

Check Point One: Stop here and get a teacher's initials
before going on to prepare your presentation:_____

FIG. 3–5: Historian's Worksheet for Detecting Information on the Renaissance

Your name:_____

Before you begin, you must choose roles for your group work. One of you will be the <u>President</u>. The job of the President is to make sure that everyone in the group helps out and that the group gets its work done on time. The job of the <u>Clerk</u> is to keep an accurate set of notes. (Everyone is also to fill in completely her or his own worksheet.) The job of the <u>Presenter</u> is to lead the group's presentation when teaching the rest of the class what you learned from your documents.

The President is_____   The Clerk is_____

The Presenter is_____

<u>Group 5</u>: Michelangelo's "David" (close-up of the head)
Pisano's "Sibyl" (detail); Verrocchio's "Lorenzo de Medici"
(You must use all three documents. For background information,
see in your text pp. 358–362.)

Adjectives, Info., Conclusions   Where you found it

Check Point One: Stop here and get a teacher's initials
before going on to prepare your presentation:_____

historians when they relied on one another. When cooperation was planned and organized—when, for example, the group read each source aloud together or divided the sources among members for individual readings—it usually made collective life easier and more enjoyable. After a group had finished drawing generalizations from their sources they turned to preparing their oral presentation. Here, just as in the first part of the project when the group's forward movement depended on the consensus worksheet, everyone in the group also had a role in the oral presentation, but the "Presenter" was responsible for organizing and planning it.

Part I of the Renaissance unit, working collaboratively as student historians from primary sources, required cooperation within each group. Part II, the oral presentation, used a "jigsaw" approach to foster cooperation *among* the six collaborative groups in the class. The essential ingredient in a jigsaw is that at some point in the project, every student has a turn as an expert whose knowledge is indispensable. Because each group had learned from different primary sources, we had six collaborative groups of resident "experts" in the room, each with competence in a different aspect of the Renaissance. What they had learned working collaboratively as student historians they would now teach the others in the class, none of whom had seen the group's primary sources or knew what that group had concluded. The final unit test was based on information from all six oral presentations. Thus the "table setting" continued rewarding students teaching students.

Of course, it was one thing to tell the kids, Go teach! and quite another for that to happen. On an earlier project the presenters had mumbled their way through their oral reports; and the students in the class had acted as if they could care less. It was painful to watch. The results of unit tests correlated well with the sloppiness of the presentations. My colleague and I decided to ask the class before we embarked on the same voyage again what the problem had been. Why did you do so poorly the last time we tried this? I asked, playing my earnest self. I'm really surprised, I told them. I know you guys are smart and capable. We need to get to the bottom of this *before* we do it again, or we'll just repeat the disaster.

After a distressingly long silence truths began to surface. The speakers had mumbled strange names, reading aloud notes that did not always make sense. They could not hear what their friends and classmates were saying. They had no real option, they felt, even though it meant failing a test. After all, you did not want to embarrass yourself or a friend by asking stupid questions no one could answer.

We all agreed that it would be good to solve this problem. We began by creating a list of basic guidelines for oral presentations. The students knew what to do, even though they had not done it: speak clearly; make eye contact; go slowly enough so that people can take notes; put names and headings on the board; and, ask for questions. Then, as a role play exercise we asked a student volunteer to mumble her way through the names of all those in her extended family while the class tried to take notes. Everyone could see the need to ask her to slow down, repeat, and put the information on the board where it could be seen as well as (not) heard. After further discussion we agreed as well that the audience has to accept some responsibility for the speaker's success. The temptation to crack up the speaker may be hard to resist. But, then, what happens when it is your turn? The class decided that listeners should be patient, encouraging, and respectful (rather than mocking), especially when someone is having a hard time.

Despite their earnest efforts and a newly raised consciousness, the kids still required intrusive coaching before and during their presentations. We were gentle and honest (or so it seemed to us!), consciously modeling the respectful attitude needed when a small community critiques itself. Yet we were also forceful. Presenters—remember, everyone in the group had to participate—did not get off the hook just because they thought they were through. Sometimes we asked for revisions and second "takes" for parts of a completed presentation. We also double checked the audience's note taking. Looking over students' shoulders, when we wondered whether students understood the words they had written, we asked them the questions we thought they needed to ask the presenters.

Grades for the group's oral presentation were based on the quality of the historical content presented and on the effectiveness of the group's teaching method. Group members shared one grade for their oral presentation. They also got written feedback about how they had done. The unit tests, on the other hand—there were two, one a traditional content-oriented test based on all six oral reports, the other an exercise that asked students to work with primary sources—were taken individually. Each student received her or his own grade. To do well on their unit tests, of course, each student was dependent on the learning and teaching skills of other students in the class. Finally, we added to all these evaluations the grade from the individual "Historian's Worksheet" that had been collected earlier. This provided a buffer, a way to give students who had difficulty with the project credit for serious effort.

COOPERATION

Watching students at work it was clear to me that what was happening was more than formal collaboration. The kids "got it"; on this history project, working together was better than working alone. Students discussed the meaning of words, often arguing from different perspectives and sometimes adopting each other's positions. Information and insights that one student provided enabled others in the group to understand a particular source. Students learned to check that everyone's conclusions were drawn from their sources. They questioned each other about incomplete or illogical statements. They argued over contradictory views. They brainstormed better ways to say what they were learning. Ideas and questions—working hypotheses—changed from day to day as the group's interactions continued.

The extent to which kids learned to care about one another's growth, whatever the level of achievement, is illustrated by what happened when I sat down with a ninth grader who was unable to draw *any* information about the Renaissance from Michelangelo's *Pietà* (Figure 3–6), one of the group's primary sources. What seems like simple analysis to a teacher can be abstract and difficult for a student who has not been asked often enough over his years in schools to think critically. The student and I talked first about how art can be a mirror reflecting its time. While that got the two of us nowhere it did catch the attention of the rest of the group. Remembering that concepts also can be learned through negative examples, I followed with a series of absurd questions. Is Michelangelo's *Pietà* about baseball? I asked. After some thought—was the question unclear? I wondered—the student said, "No." Is it about Central High? I continued . . . The shirt you are wearing? . . . The trees out the window? . . . Tomorrow's weather? Soon the "nos" came more readily. What *is* it about? was still an unanswerable puzzle for this student, however. When, finally, after the third set of absurd suggestions, the young man replied in a quizzical voice, "Religion?", his group burst into a spontaneous cheer that took both of us by surprise.

"Which religion?" I queried after the cries had died down.

"Christianity?" the ninth grader asked, studying Mary holding Jesus.

"And how do you know that?"

Pointing to Mary and Jesus, he explained *to his group* who they were.

Just as the ninth graders relied on one another, my colleague and I depended on each other, and not only for lesson ideas or to help with the hectic mechanics of in-class group work. When my colleague was discouraged and ready to throw in the towel, somehow it turned out that I saw the kids as on the verge of pulling it all together. When I felt discouraged, concerned that the quality of the students' work was low and their interest flagging, my partner helped me with his optimism that a new day and rewrites were all that were needed. When we both felt blue at the same time we waited for the next day.

Often I think teachers as well as students need collaborators. It seems only fair.

FIG. 3–6: Michelangelo's Pietà

WHERE ARE YOU NOW?

❖ *Which of the following conditions do you consider necessary for your students to work collaboratively?*

_____ students highly interested in the subject matter

_____ students have the skills they need before they begin

_____ students like the people in their group

_____ project structured by the teacher so that students need each other's help to do their work

_____ more than one teacher in the room

_____ a grading system that holds each student responsible individually and rewards students who depend on other students

_____ activities designed to involve students in their work

_____ continuing practice and experience working cooperatively

_____ other?

❖ *Which two of the conditions that you checked do you consider most important? Why?*

❖ *Can there be too much structure for group work (for example, worksheets for primary source note taking with checkpoints; group roles; jigsaw-type oral reports)? How much is too much?*

❖ *Do you think **your** students need to work collaboratively in order to act as historians (for example, generating questions, drawing valid conclusions from primary sources, reporting to others)?*

❖ *What is one thing you took from this chapter that you might apply now in your classroom?*

❖ *What issues you think are important were not raised in this chapter?*

NOTES

1. Two helpful group work "primers" are Susan Ellis and Susan Whalen, *Cooperative Learning* (New York: Scholastic Press, 1993); and David Johnson, Roger Johnson, and Edyth Holubec, *The New Circles of Learning: Cooperation in the Classroom and School* (Alexandria, VA: ASCD, 1994).

2. See Chapter 2 for a more complete version of this lesson.

4

Simple Rules

THE BEST HISTORIANS IN THE WORLD

The student historian approach invited students to value the histories they constructed rather than rely on the history created by generations of trained professionals. Even now, the enormity of this dream takes my breath away. What arrogance to think that the products of school kids—their definition of essential historical questions, their selection from available source materials, their determination of topics, the conclusions they drew and presented—could replace, even temporarily, the work of the best historians in the world.

The list of skills, attitudes, and habits of mind needed for historical work is formidable. A historian, for example, must be able to

- read and comprehend, including understanding archaic vocabulary
- discover the main idea(s) in a piece of writing
- understand the importance of perspective and context, including using internal and external evidence to check the validity of a source
- develop a sense of the importance of time and time passing: what generalizations are (and are not) supportable by historical evidence
- synthesize, that is, see themes, or patterns, in a set of primary materials
- write clearly and persuasively and present ideas orally
- revise hypotheses as fresh information requires
- work collaboratively as part of a community of historians
- exercise intellectual honesty and integrity

For mainstreamed ESL students and recent immigrants for whom English is not a first language, as for native-born students who test below reading grade level, finding the main idea in a paragraph in an English language history textbook can be a challenge. Even though we are not attempting to train future professional historians—our goal is to educate children and young adults—students who work extensively with primary sources will have to practice the complex skills of the historian. Otherwise teachers and students will wind up with half-baked presentations masquerading as serious history.

What is the best way for students to learn the skills they need?

Graduate students in the social sciences and humanities spend two or three years in extensive study before they begin their dissertations. Such training in "research" methods is clearly impossible in middle and high schools: we would always be getting started and we would never "finish."

Traditional models of teaching skills usually suggest a sequential approach, beginning with the basics and proceeding to increasingly complicated and demanding combinations. We certainly did our share of explaining and modeling, followed by student practice and assessment (feedback). But the results were usually mixed. Many students successfully completed the test exercises, but when they encountered an opportunity to apply the skills in other situations, few seemed to realize that what they had learned were problem-solving tools they could choose voluntarily. It was as if the skill-building lessons had a life of their own that was separate from all else.

Progress in the development of students' "research" skills usually followed quite a different path. The skills *needed* to do a project are also intricate parts of *doing* the project. They are best learned in the process of struggling with the project. In other words, we came to see the development of skills as part of the project, rather than preparation for it. We could not separate *working* as a student historian from *learning how* to work as a student historian. Imagine trying to learn to ride a bicycle solely by reading a manual and practicing pedal strokes in the air.

As a result, we faced a planning problem. In general, I believe it is unfair for teachers to expect kids to know what they have yet to study. Relying on students' out-of-school experiences means rewarding and penalizing what kids bring to class rather than what they do in class. At the same time, if the skills needed are taught and learned in process, then where do you begin? What constitutes an entry point that does not ask students to know what they have yet to study?

SIMPLE RULES

I began to understand better how students could "learn while doing" as I read about artificial intelligence.

Let us say, for the sake of an analogy, that I am the Grand Prize Winner in the "Twenty-First Century Sweepstakes." My prize? A design team of former NASA engineers is to build me a set of robots that will automatically vacuum my home for the rest of my life. All I need do is supply an accurate topographic map.

Ah, . . . wait a minute, I say, graph paper and sharpened pencil in hand. How "accurate" does this map have to be? Does it need the "exact" distance from the throw rug in the hall by the front door to the wall? The exact height of the risers on the carpeted stairs to the nearest, what, tenth of an inch? What if the middle of each step is slightly worn by years of use? And once I submit my map, can I never again move tables and chairs or let children into the house? (Will the robot try to vacuum the cat when it hides under the couch?)

My point is that specific, "map-type" computer programs can never be detailed enough, no matter how detailed. Eventually, the robot always comes up against something that is not exactly according to plan. Simulated models are neither as complex nor as mercurial as the real world.

The NASA specialists who built mobile robot species for the moon landing in 1969 early on switched to an approach that allowed robots to make their own decisions. The NASA engineers created what can be called a "simple rule" computer program that, in effect, let robots "think" for themselves as they encountered new situations on the lunar surface. Instead of a precise topographic map, the program that worked best was a set of basic guidelines that dictated how to respond to whatever was in the environment. A typical rule might state that when the robot is traveling in a straight line, if the right edge comes within a prescribed distance from a solid, it should reverse half its length, turn five degrees to the left, and try again. Similarly, the intricate patterns of birds in flight may also be an example of complex behavior based on simple guideline rules, but this time, rules that are probably genetically endowed. Each bird defines a certain space around it and then constantly maneuvers to keep the distance between itself and the birds in front, in back, to the left, and to the right intact.

Life on the moon proved too complicated for an inflexible program in the robot's "head." Student historians also need *not* a "map" of how to proceed but guideline "rules" in order to adapt to the unforeseen and unimagined. As new questions surface, these simple rules suggest ways they can develop alternative paths worth considering. Practice then becomes learning.

We developed for our students our own version of the basic work rules historians generally follow in their research and writing: 1) have access to a representative range of accurate information about your subject (currently available technology can easily change that to "a broad and representative range"); 2) use this information in your work (all conclusions must be based on it); and 3) do not say anything that is contradicted by information to which you have access. In short, have accurate sources; use them; don't abuse them.

We worked hard to make the application of these rules the accepted norm in our classroom community. We encouraged students to use them to solve problems that surfaced. But, as is usual in teaching and learning, our actual experience was more nuanced. One does not simply explain guidelines to students and expect them to begin, and continue, working unassisted. This "simple rules" approach to learning skills always operated within a complicated support structure that included introductory involvement activities; document analysis worksheets; written prompts to help students organize their work; collaborative groups; teacher coaching (while resisting students' insistent pleas for the "correct" answer); peer editing; modeling by students and teachers; oral and written feedback from students and teachers; constant encouragement; and grades. And at least half the time, there were two adults in the room. (For more on the importance of partners and allies, see Chapter 1.)

Despite the familiar sound to the support structure, the "simple rules" approach to teaching skills leads to a different, deeper kind of learning than more traditional skill-building models. The basic rules did not include a list of "correct" techniques for solving common problems historians face. What they provided instead were guidelines for figuring out solutions to problems, including those students had not encountered before. The "simple rules" approach, to quote a beginning teacher I worked with, expects "kids to appreciate the power of their own minds."[1] I like to think of these simplified rules, at their best, as a "teacher within each student." When building complex skills from simple rules, students tell themselves how to proceed, while the teacher acts as mentor and advisor to the novice historians. Once students were using the building block rules regularly—almost "automatically"—they used the guidelines virtually to teach themselves.

How did the kids start working as historians with complicated primary sources? Where was the best entry point to an intellectually demanding unit, given that, like everyone else, students cannot "do" what they do not already "know"?

It was not with skills lessons. Instead, we began at the beginning, with student involvement, to evoke the energy and intensity they would need to learn and carry out the work required. After the involvement activities, we usually presented the simple rules orally, wrote them on the board, and explained them using analogous examples from the kids' lives. It was only then that they were introduced to primary sources, and always with a partner or in a collaborative group. In the final analysis, it was by struggling *together* that students developed their research skills as historians.

HERE I STAND: TEACHING SKILLS

❖ *How do students usually learn the skills they need in your classroom?*

　　____ come in with them
　　____ from discrete lessons taught in class prior to the project that
　　　　 requires the skills
　　____ in the process of doing the project that requires the skills
　　____ by following a "simple rules" approach
　　____ other ways?

❖ *Have you used the "simple rules lead to complex work" method in your teaching? If you have, what would be an example? What were the advantages of using this approach? What were the problems that needed solutions?*

❖ *Do you agree that a "simple rules" approach encourages kids to "appreciate the power of their own minds," a kind of learning they do not necessarily achieve when they are taught skills through discrete lessons designed for that purpose? Do you have any comments to add?*

❖ *Can you think of other examples, in your own life or from your reading, in which simple steps led to large consequences down the road?*

FROM THE CLASSROOM:
THE UNITED STATES FIGHTS WARS

"The United States Fights Wars," a collaboratively planned unit taught to students at three schools, included sources from the War of 1812 through the 1991 Gulf War. I offer it here as a classroom example to illustrate a "simple rules" approach to learning skills.

When I introduced students to the project, I always emphasized that this unit was not purely "academic."[2] It was about *them*, I told the students. Our study of history can help you think through what it is that you would be willing to die for, and what it is you would be willing to kill for. Do you think war will stop in your lifetime? I asked. Then, rather than turn immediately to historical background information, we took the kids through two days of "writing for thinking" exercises and classroom "plaza" walking activities. These were intended to stress two important points: that all historians write from a values perspective and that the students' values strongly influence how they understand, evaluate, and use or ignore the history they study in school. Then, after a brief lesson on how knowledge of the past can help answer current, pressing questions, we turned to the simple guidelines for working as a historian.

I wrote our three aphorisms, "have accurate information; use it; don't abuse it," on the board, explained that they were essential working rules for this project, and amplified these ideas through discussion and examples. Concrete illustrations from the kids' lives helped make the abstractions clear. For instance, we were all sitting in a second-floor classroom, so to claim that the school was designed on one level for the convenience of tired teachers and students is a clear abuse of the information we have access to. That statement ignores information we know is accurate. Historians cannot do that even when they "know" the point of the statement, that the school was designed with the interest of teachers and students in mind, is accurate. In validating conclusions we rely on accurate information. We do not ignore stuff for the sake of convenience. Valid evidence is the key; without sources we can come to no conclusions. In some classes we also added an exercise on how students made decisions about a range of important questions in their own lives: What "sources" do they rely on? How do they know—or do they care—if that information is accurate? Are there decisions so personal it is best just to jump without examining what you know or how you know it?

The introductory activities for "The United States Fights Wars" unit—writing for thinking exercises, classroom "plaza" walking activities, using history to answer current questions, how kids make decisions, and introducing simple rules for student historians—usually took the opening two or three classes. We saw those lessons as the necessary preamble to the unit. Without them, success was less likely.

The following day, either lesson three or four of the unit, we placed three identical stacks of photocopied primary source documents on the floor in the front of the room. (The stacks would not remain in order for long!) We began with a quick review of what we had accomplished so far. Then we passed out a "Master List of Documents" (see Figure 4–1) to each student. The list divided the thirty-nine primary sources (the stacks on the floor) according to categories we had created, such as "What Our Leaders Said" and "The Role of Newspapers." Each document on the master list had a descriptive title (for example, "General Jackson Calls for Black Volunteers [1814]" or "The Anglo-Saxon Mission [1885]") along with letters and numbers that indicated specific wars. Although we had selected and arranged particular documents, thus making some significant decisions about definition and interpretation *before* students began working, it seemed a necessary compromise if the class was not to collapse in frustration. Almost without exception, students needed these written prompts to help them organize their work.

At this point we divided some classes into collaborative working groups

FIG. 4–1: Master List of Documents (The United States Fights Wars)

The Role of Blacks in Wars:

A. 2   General Jackson calls for Black volunteers (1814)
C. 1   Draft Riots in New York City (1863)
F. 3   Black Americans return home from fighting for freedom (1919)
F. 6   Leaders at Versailles (1919)

What Our Leaders Said:

A. 1   Henry Clay's speech (1816)
D. 1   Should America annex the Philippines? (1899)
D. 4   The President decides to annex the Philippines (1898)
D. 5   The "Anglo-Saxon Mission" (1885)
D. 7   In favor of American imperialism
E. 1   President Roosevelt's claims (1904)
E. 2   Dollar Diplomacy
F. 2   Why America fought in World War I (1917)
F. 4   Propaganda posters (1918)
F. 5   Merchants of Death (1934)
G. 3   The decision to drop the atomic bomb on Hiroshima (1945)
H. 1   The Gulf of Tonkin "incident" (1964)
I. 1   Herman Kahn thinks the unthinkable (1962)

The Role of Newspapers:

A. 3   Editorial in the *Washington National Intelligencer* (1812)
D. 2   Front page of the *New York World* (1898)
H. 6   How America goes to war (1991)

The Action of Wars:

B. 4   Custer's last stand (1876)
B. 5   The Sand Creek Massacre
C. 2   A Confederate soldier (1861)
C. 4   Letter from a Union soldier (1863)
C. 5   Battle of Antietam described (1862)
D. 3   Torture (1898)
D. 6   Preparing for battle (1898)
F. 1   From a nurse's diary (1918)
G. 1   On a beachhead in Italy (1943)
G. 4   On the beach after D-Day (1944)
H. 2   Execution of a prisoner
H. 3; H. 4; H. 5: Letters home from soldiers in Vietnam

Opponents' Points of View:

B. 1   Yuma's way of life (1905)
B. 2   Tecumseh's speech to General Harrison (1810)
B. 3   A Pawnee scout speaks (1879)
C. 3   Sherman's march through the South (1864)
G. 2   Relocation of Japanese Americans (1940's)

continued next page

FIG. 4–1: Master List of Documents, continued

KEY: A. documents are about the War of 1812
        B.   describe wars with the "Indians"
        C.   are about the Civil War (1861-1865)
        D.   are about the Spanish-American War (1898)
        E.   are about wars with Latin Americans
        F.   are about World War I
        G.   are about World War II
        H.   describe the war in Vietnam
        I.   is about the possibility of nuclear war

of four or five. Using the Master List as their introductory guide, the kids chose documents and began working as student historians. The simple rules served as guidelines for how to proceed, and the teachers acted as coaches and mentors when, inevitably, problems developed and questions arose.

More often, however, we began with a smaller bite. Students chose a partner, or, when they insisted, worked in a triad with two others. The students perused the Master List and from that limited information selected any two documents they wanted to look at, for whatever reason. We encouraged them to browse among these pieces of "accurate information." It should be much like flipping through a magazine while waiting in a clinic or a doctor's office, we said. Just pick out a document that catches your eye.

Once students had settled on their documents and become interested in what they had chosen, we passed around copies of the "Background Worksheet for Documents" (Figure 4–2). This worksheet was intended to help students understand how historians study sources. It also gave them practice in applying the simple rule, *use* accurate information. Working with their partner or in their triad, students used these worksheets to cull significant information from the documents they had selected. For those who were unsure about how to find the main idea, for example, or how to identify the speaker's perspective, the worksheet could serve as a novice's guide. To that extent it was successful. Often, however, kids began the unit by filling out background worksheets for every document they read, as if the worksheet was the final product they would show the teacher (after all, filling out worksheets on a "text" is a common school practice, often an end in itself). Fortunately, as students became more familiar with the process and understood what was expected of them, we dropped the worksheet structure.

When partners had completed their basic analysis of the sources they had chosen at random, we placed the students in collaborative work groups of four, five, and sometimes six. The composition of the groups depended

FIG. 4–2: The United States Fights Wars: Background Worksheet for Documents

Your name: _____

1. Our Document # is: _____ Name of Document:_____

2. Names of important people mentioned; who they were; why they were important:
   NAME of Person   WHO she or he was   WHY IMPORTANT

3. Places mentioned; where they were; why they were important:
   NAME of Place   WHERE it is   WHY IMPORTANT

4. Difficult words:
   WORD   Usable DEFINITION

5. Who is the narrator, or speaker, of your source?

6. The Larger Picture: What's going on at this time that you need to know about in order to understand this document?

on the size of the class and the classroom teacher's judgment about which students would work best together. Since each student brought two already analyzed documents into the group, a group of four began with eight sources (although some might, by chance, be "duplicates"). The first collaborative task for the newly formed group was to discover a common theme among these eight sources.

Finding a common theme even for a limited set of primary sources that had been chosen on the basis of personal interest turned out to be difficult. We tried a variety of techniques to help students see patterns. The most amusing (for me if not for the students) was an approach we borrowed from "Sesame Street." Which of these documents go together, we asked (but did not sing), and which don't belong with the others? We also asked prompt-type questions, suggested analogies from the students' own lives, and asked questions that probed for deeper meanings hidden within students' initial responses. Whatever the technique, our goal was to encourage brainstorming within the group. We trusted that students from diverse backgrounds knew more and, especially when working collaboratively, were capable of much more than they realized.

When the members of a group stopped in frustration, unable to find a common thread that made sense to them, we suggested that they choose five, or four, or even just three documents that seemed connected. The group then formed a "tentative hypothesis" for this highly reduced "data base" and again using the Master List as a guide, hunted for other documents that might fit.

As the frustration level built, we felt it important to encourage students. After all, many had not encountered this way of studying history before. How were they to know that the learning process has its natural ups and downs? Hang in there, we told them. If you are feeling confused, you are in exactly the right place. Anyone who claims that being responsible for serious thinking is easy is just wrong.

Sometimes, when a number of groups could not see a common theme among their sources, we decided to interrupt their work and model the learning process. Using primary sources from "The United States Fights Wars" document pack, we suggested a variety of ways these documents could be related and analyzed each step as we took it. Yet often such modeling was not immediately helpful. The kids had to struggle with their task themselves until, often quite suddenly, they understood how to do it.

Once a group agreed on a tentative hypothesis and had it okayed by a teacher, they returned to the Master List, or directly to the piles of paper on the floor, to find other documents—seven to ten items, depending on the class—which would support or amplify the theme they had generated from their originals. They had chosen the first primary sources according to their own individual interests. Now they looked specifically for related sources. As they added more primary sources, the additional information and new points of view often required that they revise their thinking, because student historians cannot "abuse" what they know. Often those revisions were a product of extended discussions that carried over from one day to the next. Sometimes, there were hurt feelings. Whatever it took, in all instances students wrote their mini-histories collaboratively. In several classes some groups also made oral presentations, to their class or to other classes.

❖ *In your opinion, is "The United States Fights Wars" unit a classroom example of learning and teaching skills by the "simple rules" approach? Your comment?*

It is important, I think, to sample a "history" from this unit. The proof of the pudding, after all, is never the recipe. If we begin with tenth graders, in this case mainstreamed ESL students who are studying history for the first time as student historians who rely on primary sources, what should we expect to see?

What we should expect to see is not something that closely resembles the polished paper of a college history major; nor are other high schoolers' essays, like those published in the *Concord Review*, a suitable comparison. That admirable enterprise, and others like it,[3] requires a mastery of language and style, and an interest in academic history, that puts it out of reach, at least initially, for most of today's middle and high school students. But our goal was neither to train the future historians of the world nor to emulate the finished products of professionals. What we are about is general education. What we hope for is that students, whatever their personal history or acquired skill level, will come to appreciate the potential power of their minds. And, since practice (with appropriate feedback) can be a powerful way to learn, as time passes and if students stay with their history projects, their writing skills improve.

The sample student "history" from the "Wars" project is reprinted as written, with spelling errors and grammatical problems intact. The difficulties students had in expressing themselves in "standard" English may surprise some readers, depending on their teaching experiences; but when I first saw this essay I was elated. It seemed a marvelous success story, a prime example of students using their minds well. I think it is important for us to recognize that many students can use their minds very well, even if their writing skills lag behind.

Among the students' accomplishments:

- Creating and developing an interesting hypothesis from their reading of previously unseen primary sources.
- Validating all statements and conclusions by referring to documents. (Copies of several of the sources the students consulted are also reprinted.)
- Reading and understanding documents and then analyzing them within their historical context (before the project these students usually had low scores on objective-type history tests).
- Thinking developmentally and writing with intellectual honesty and integrity.
- Writing history with the readers' needs in mind.
- Working collaboratively; that is, developing their knowledge in a social context.

In the many wars the United States has been involved in each has shown a great deal of torture whether it was mental or Physical torture. Throughout this paper we will show you evidence proving the torturing of our soldiers and our enemies soldiers. First we will discuss situations of physical torture. Then, we will continue to tell you about the mental torture soldiers go through.

During the Spanish-American war a former corpral named Daniel J. Evans witnessed a torture known as "water Cure." This torture was done to insurgents by Americans. It was used to get them to tell whether the rest of the insurgents were. The infamation here was found In a Testimony of a former Corpral Daniel J. Evans D-3. The mistreatment of Japanese Americans was another form of torture. Innocent Japanese Americans who where "Loyal" citizens of the United States where taken away from there homes and jobs and placed relocation camps. Document G-2 The relocation of Japanese American tells us that while living in these camps Janese America were treated badly. For Ex. They could have visitors but could only visit through a fence under the watchful eyes of guards. Document D-2 Shows a South Veitnamiese general shooting a man accused of being on the other side. It is a Saigon scene during the test offense. Shortly after the American Public was shocked to hear the Americans troops had killed Some 300 civilians most were women + children. The behavior of soldiers was another form of torture.

The physicall torture that war can cause is of course very serious but the mental torture is also harmful. I think that in every war the U.S. has been in there has been in there has been Mental torture. Even, on Dec. 24, 1864 after

Sherman's march through the south men and women in the South faced the torture of knowing they had lost everything. This was found on Document C-3 Sherman's March. In Document D-5 a soldier who is writing home tells his friend that he has not been physically harmed but he now knows that a man is not sick unless he is enjoying the sickness of the war. This is Document H-3 Is another letter sent from a Marine named Kevin back to his parents. In this letter he tells his parents how seriously dangerous the battle is. He says that after losing his best friend he is still not physically harmed but has gone through a great deal of pain and matured greatly. More letters from soldiers such as G-4 and C-4 tell of more mental torture but not only soldiers who are fighting know of this pain. Document F-1 is taken from a nurses diary. This document tells us pain and torture a nurse feels after losing a patient. Although the nurse wenth through this many times she said that she could not stop the tears.

We think that there was a change in the treatment of soldiers physcially but mentally nothing can be changed. Document F-5 tells us that to kill a soldier it cost about 25,000 but we have decided no matter what the cost is we would not fight in a war.

EXAMPLES OF FOUR PRIMARY SOURCES STUDENTS USED TO WRITE THEIR HISTORY

C.3   Sherman's March: A Southern View

Sherman's march though Georgia and the Carolinas inflicted terrible destruction on those states. In the following reading, 24-year-old Eliza Frances Andrews records the devastation she saw in central Georgia.

December 24, 1864 - About three miles from Sparta we struck the "burnt country," as it is well named by the natives, and then I could better understand the wrath and desperation of these poor people. I almost felt as if I should like to hang a Yankee myself. There was hardly a fence left standing all the way from Sparta to Gordon. The fields were trampled down and the road was lined with carcasses of horses, hogs, and cattle that the invaders, unable either to consume or to carry away with them, had wantonly shot down, to starve out the people and prevent them from making their crops. The stench in some places was unbearable; every few hundred yards we had to hold our noses or stop them with the cologne Mrs. Elzey had given us, and it proved a great boon. The dwellings that were standing all showed signs of pillage, and on every plantation we saw the charred remains of the ginhouse and packing screw, while here and there lone chimney stacks, "Sherman's sentinels," told of homes laid in ashes.

The infamous wretches! I couldn't wonder now that these poor people should want to put a rope round the neck of every red-handed "devil of them" they could lay their hands on. Hayricks and fodder stacks were demolished, corncribs were empty, and every bale of cotton that could be found was burnt by the savages. . . . Before crossing the Oconee at Milledgeville we ascended an immense hill, from which there was a fine view of the town, with Governor Brown's fortifications in the foreground and the river rolling at our feet. The Yankees had burnt the bridge; so we had to cross on a ferry. There was a long train of vehicles ahead of us, and it was nearly an hour before our turn came; so we had ample time to look about us.

On our left was a field where 30,000 Yankees had camped hardly three weeks before. It was strewn with the debris they had left behind, and the poor people of the neighborhood were wandering over it, seeking for anything they could find to eat, even picking up grains of corn that were scattered around where the Yankees had fed their horses. We were told that a great many valuables were found there at first, plunder that the invaders had left behind, but the place had been picked over so often by this time that little now remained except tufts of loose cotton, piles of half-rotted grain, and the carcasses of slaughtered animals, which raised a horrible stench. Some men were plowing in one part of the field, making ready for next year's crop.

❖ ❖ ❖ ❖ ❖ ❖ ❖ ❖ ❖

H. 3   A Letter Home

29 January 68
Dear Mom and Dad,
I guess by now you are worried sick over my safety. Khe Sanh village was overrun, but not the combat base. The base was hit and hit hard by artillery, mortars and rockets. All my gear and the rest of the company's gear was destroyed. Right now we are living in bunkers just like the Marines at Con Thien did last fall.

I am unhurt and have not been touched. I skinned my knee on the initial assault, but other than that I am OK. My morale is not the best because my best buddy was killed the day before yesterday. I was standing about 20 feet from him and a 60-mm mortar exploded next to him. He caught a piece of shrapnel in the head. I carried him over to the aid station where he died. I cried my eyes out. I have seen death before but nothing as close as this. Junior, my buddy, had 67 days left in country and then he was to return to his wife and daughter. His death really hit me hard. Two days before that four other Marines in my company were killed by a rocket exploding on the floor of their bunker. They were killed instantly, but their bodies were horribly mangled. I think with all the death and destruction I have seen in the past week I have aged greatly. I feel like an old man now. I am not as happy-go-lucky as before, and I think more maturely now. Payback for my buddies is not the uppermost thought in my mind. My biggest goal is to return to you and Dad and Ann in June or July.

The battle for Khe Sanh is not over yet. Since it began, we (Bravo Company, 3rd Recon Battalion) have lost 14 men KIA and 44 men WIA. Our company is cut down to half strength, and I think we will be going to Okinawa to regroup. I hope so anyway because I have seen enough of war and its destruction. I am scarred by it but not scared enough to quit. I am a Marine and I hope someday to be a good one. Perhaps that way I can be worthy of the friendship Junior and I shared. It bothers me to think of these so-called Americans who shirk their responsibility to our country. If I even get close enough to a peace picket, he will see part of the Vietnam War in my eyes. They cannot compare to the man Junior was. I will miss him greatly. He was with me since June of last year, and we went everywhere together. We have so little over here, but we share it all.

Please pray for us all here at Khe Sanh and also for my buddy Junior Reather. I hope he is happy where he is. Take care and God Bless.

> Your Son & Marine,
> Kevin

D. 3 Testimony of Former Corporal Daniel J. Evans

THE CHAIRMAN: The committee would like to hear from you concerning the conduct of the war. Did you witness any cruelties inflicted upon the natives of the Philippine Islands, and if so, under what circumstances?

ANSWER: The case I had reference to was where they gave the water cure to a native in the Ilicano Province of Ilocos Norte.

QUESTION: That is in the extreme northern part of Luzon?

ANSWER: Yes, sir. There were two native scouts that were with the American forces. They went out and brought in a couple of insurgents. There were known to be insurgents by their own confession. Besides that, they had the mark that most insurgents in that part of the country carry. It is a little brand on the left breast, generally inflicted with a nail or head of a cartridge. They tried to find out from this native—

QUESTION: What kind of a brand did you say it was?

ANSWER: A small brand put on with a nail head or cartridge.

SEN. BEVERIDGE: A scar on the flesh?

THE WITNESS: Yes, sir. They tried to get him to tell where the rest of the insurgents were at that time. We knew about where they were, but we did not know how to get at them. They were in the hills, and it happened that there was only one path that could get to them. They refused to tell this one path and they commenced this so-called "water cure." The first thing one of the Americans did—I mean one of the scouts for the Americans—was to grab one of the men by the head and jerk his head back. Then they took a tomato can and poured water down his throat until he could hold no more. During this time one of the natives had a rattan whip, about as large as my finger. He struck him on the face and on the bare back. Every time they would strike him it would raise a large welt, and some blood would come. When this native could hold no more water, they forced a gag into his mouth. They stood him up and tied his hands behind him. They stood him up against a post and fastened him so he could not move. Then one man, an American soldier, who was over six feet tall, and who was very strong, too, struck this native in the pit of the stomach. He hit him as hard as he could strike him, just as rapidly as he could. It seemed as if he didn't get tired of striking him.

SEN. ALLISON: With his hand?

ANSWER: With his clenched fist. He struck him right in the pit of the stomach and it made the native very sick. They kept that operation up for quite a time. I thought the fellow was about to die, but I don't believe he was as bad as that, because finally he told them he would tell. He was taken away, and I saw no more of him.

QUESTION: Did he tell?

ANSWER: I believe he did, because I didn't hear of any more water cure inflicted on him.

SEN. RAWLINS: Was there any effort to conceal it?

ANSWER: Not in the least.

QUESTION: Was it a matter of common knowledge?

ANSWER: Yes, sir, it has been the talk of almost the whole army. They do not try to conceal it.

QUESTION: How long has that been the case?

ANSWER: Well, it has been practiced, to my knowledge, from along in July 1900 until the time I left the islands. Of course, after that time I knew nothing about it. I left the islands about February 1901.

❖ ❖ ❖ ❖ ❖ ❖ ❖ ❖ ❖

F. 1   Behind the Lines
Entries from the diary of an American nurse, 1918

April 1st

The big drive is over and the terrific rush has stopped, at least temporarily, but the hospital is still filled.

Most of the men are too badly wounded to be moved, although we need the space, for we are swamped with influenza cases. I thought influenza was a bad cold, something like the grippe, but this is much worse than that. These men run a high temperature, so high that we can't believe it's true, and often take it again to be sure. It is accompanied by vomiting and dysentery. When they die, as about half of them do, they turn a ghastly dark gray and are taken out at once and cremated.

We are better organized now, and able to keep track of pulses and temperatures, and we have some system. There are special wards for the influenza, one for gangrene cases, another one for major gas burns, one for meningitis, one for fractures, one for spinal injuries, and so on. I have worked in all of them and cannot make up my mind which is the worst.

November 8th

More and more Americans in the death ward [a ward where dying cases are quartered]. Gas cases are terrible. They cannot breathe lying down or sitting up. They just struggle for breath, but nothing can be done . . . their lungs are gone. . . . [Some are] covered with first degree burns. We try to relieve them by pouring oil on them. They cannot be bandaged or even touched. We cover them with a tent of propped-up sheets. Gas burns must be agonizing because usually the other cases do not complain even with the worst of wounds. But gas cases invariably are beyond endurance and they cannot help crying out. . . .

November 10th

Charley [an American sergeant who was almost completely paralyzed] died this morning. I held his hand as he went and could not keep back the tears. Near the end he saw me crying and patted my hand with his two living fingers to comfort me. I cannot describe that boy's sweetness. He took part of my heart with him. Everybody around the place was in tears.

Just after he went someone came into the ward and said: "Armistice! The staff cars have just passed by the gate on their way to Senlis to sign an Armistice!"

What a time and place to come in shouting about an Armistice! I said: "Sh! Sh!"

There is no armistice for Charley or for any of the others in that ward.

One of the boys began to sob. I went and talked soothingly to him, but what could I say, knowing he would die before night?

Well, it's over. I have to keep telling myself, it's over, it's over, it's over.

But there is still that letter to write to Charley's mother. I can hear commotion and shouting through the hospital as I write this. The chapel bell is ringing wildly.

I am glad it is over, but my heart is heavy as lead. Must write that letter.

One of the girls came looking for me. They have opened champagne for the staff in the dining hall. I told her to get out.

Can't seem to pull myself together.

❖ ❖ ❖ ❖ ❖ ❖ ❖ ❖ ❖

NOW THAT YOU HAVE SAMPLED THE STUDENTS' HISTORY, WHAT DO YOU THINK?

❖ *As far as you can tell without having seen the class, does the students' history illustrate that they have learned the skills needed to work as student historians with primary sources? For example,*

> *Are all the students' conclusions based on primary sources from their data base?*
>
> *Is there a clear and worthwhile hypothesis, developed by the students, that grew out of their reading of primary sources?*
>
> *Is there evidence of higher-level thinking—raising significant questions, defining solvable problems, analyzing written materials, synthesizing— behind the spelling errors and awkward grammar?*
>
> *Is there evidence of collaborative work—of the development of ideas in a social context?*
>
> *Is the history written with the readers' needs in mind?*

WHAT THE STUDENTS THOUGHT

Each time we completed a "Wars" project we asked for feedback from the students. Sometimes it took the form of a discussion, and sometimes we asked for private written comments. In several classes we did both.

Following is a sampling of students' written comments, which speak to the issues raised in this chapter. All are quotations.

It went ok—it wasn't all that hard. . . .

It was fun.

I really liked working with a group, because what I don't understand, someone in the group can help me. . . .

I learned that we also have a say in history.

I understand how the text book might have been written. . . .

I felt like we were writing history and when we look at the history book our work was going to be there.

It made me feel like I went back in time and stopped at each place. . . .

When you do something you've never done before it makes it easier the next time.

You can do something if you put your mind to it—At the beginning I thought that this was going to be a disaster. Being a historian is not easy.

I know more than I thought. . . .

NOTES

1. This apt phrase is taken, with permission, from my student Annie Leonard's 1993 self-analysis of her own student teaching, East Providence High School, East Providence, Rhode Island.

2. See Chapter 2 for a more detailed account of involvement activities for this unit.

3. For example, the "convention" described by Donald G. Morrison in "Students as Historians: A Convention," *Perspectives*, Oct. 1987 was attended only by AP European history classes in suburban Westchester County, New York.

5

The Essential Enterprise

TEACHING WITH GRADES

Teaching requires a repertoire of evaluation and assessment methods, each with its own purpose. Evaluation is a task almost all classroom teachers face. With few exceptions, students must be given grades.

As a high school teacher I learned about evaluation, assessment, and grading from my own mistakes. I used to grade essay tests, for instance, by picking from the pile those essays I thought would be strongest. Assuming that a student's past performance was a reliable guide, I let the star performers in each class set my expectations for the entire class. The kids' work was inconsistent enough, of course, that eventually a little bell went off in my head telling me something was wrong. I was stumbling across too many essays from the pack that were more impressive than my pace setters. When I braved going public with my problem, another teacher in my school suggested that before I start to grade I make a list of the ideas and information I thought should be in the essay. Then I could judge all essays equally, based on my written criteria.

Once I adopted that technique, however, I realized that I could do more. If I shared my evaluation criteria with the students *before* they took their tests, instead of thinking of my list as something private, it could help them learn what I wanted them to know. "Teaching to the test" was a good idea, it seemed to me, when the test demanded what was most important and valuable. But how to give the kids the criteria for grading their essays without giving away the questions—or the answers?

At the time, I solved my problem by devising questions that lacked "correct," memorizable answers. On a midterm exam, for example, I asked an eleventh-grade U.S. history class to define "capitalism" by describing how it actually worked in the United States during the period from the Constitutional Convention to the end of Reconstruction. I told them that they had to back up their statements with references to specific historical events, that they could use only material we had covered in class, that they should beware of anachronistic thinking, and, that their answer had to be logically organized and clearly written. With an essay test like that, discussing the question in class in detail before the exam—something that proved absolutely necessary—meant extending our study of history rather than giving students answers to a test.

At that point in my growth as a teacher I could understand what others were getting at when they talked about evaluation as an integrated part of the curriculum. I perked up my ears when I heard other teachers and educators talking about using evaluation to foster learning rather than simply to assign grades. If the students were given test questions or final projects, including evaluation criteria, at the start of the unit, then they would have an outline—a kind of scaffolding, really—for upcoming work.[1] It could help kids organize the mass of material about to come their way. I liked the idea that evaluation, including grades, and the curriculum could become one, making learning and grading inseparable. I skipped down this rose-filled path, smelling the flowers and getting well scratched by the thorns.

Watching students work as historians in city schools, I came to realize something else I had not recognized before: grades can be used to mold the way students learn. That may seem obvious. After all, is it any different from saying that "tests guide the curriculum"?

I mean that, and something more than that. Grades can be a powerful teaching instrument, prompting kids to focus on the process by which they learn. (In practice, of course, the prompt does not always produce the desired response.) I tend to picture the relationship between evaluation and not what, but *how* students learn as a continuum. At their best, grades can encourage the cultivation of thoughtfulness among students; or, the evaluation system can reward quiet attentiveness and rote memory. Many choices lie between the extremes.

Teachers usually exercise only local control over the tests their students take. Unfortunately for those of us who advocate a greater reliance on a constructivist, primary-source-based approach to learning history, much history testing today encourages a quiet attentiveness and rote memorization that, unchallenged, sounds the death knell for higher-level thinking. The questions devised by history test makers often assume that the past is already accurately known. Straightforward, memory-type questions follow from that premise: If the history we want students to know is an "objective" and "accurate" story, why not check whether students have learned the correct answer?[2]

This "check-for-the-correct-answer" syndrome also applies to more sophisticated assessments that accept the existence of divergent views. Questions often ask no more of students than to repeat what the text, or classroom readings, or the teacher have said. Take a classic "compare and contrast" question that generations of students have struggled with: Compare and contrast the social and economic differences among the three (or four) major geographic sections in colonial America.

It *sounds* as if higher-level thinking is required. How can students "compare and contrast" without analyzing data and drawing conclusions based on that data? Indeed, the folks who created the National History Standards label this question an example of higher-level thinking.[3] In actuality, however, what is required falls far short of analyzing data to draw conclusions. It is not as if students have been sorting through data bases to come up with their own ideas. All that most students know about geographic areas in the colonial period is what they have read in their texts or heard from their teachers. Answering this question requires memorizing and repeating the appropriate (complex) information that others have told the student. Or, to choose a second example, what, really, is asked of students who write about the causes of the Civil War? Delving into that problem *as a historian* can be a lifetime work. For students in school, it means memorizing and repeating, for a test, the information as it was organized and presented in their textbook or by their teacher.

When it comes to learning, of course, we can never fully escape from the possession of content, nor should we want to. It is impossible to think without knowing some content to think about. Yet for students to learn higher-level thinking skills—analyzing, synthesizing, comparing and contrasting, evaluating, generating questions, and solving problems—they need test questions that ask them to move beyond memory. They need an evaluation "system" that requires each student to go through the process of learning and practicing how to think and solve problems as if it were a brand new path, and for each individual, it is. No one can "develop" thinking skills for someone else. "Understanding," "memorizing," or "copying" what someone else thought is not the same.

Middle and high school students are much more likely to develop higher-level thinking skills when the evaluation process encourages significant involvement in creating the knowledge they are studying, even if little that is novel results from their efforts. If we want higher-level thinking, earning a "good" grade should depend on participation in generating questions and searching for valid, satisfying "answers." And since, with rare exceptions, knowledge is created in social contexts, the evaluation scaffolding should ensure that collaboration is fundamental: students need one another to succeed.

For too many students, the "essential enterprise" of school is to get "good" grades or to get at least good enough grades not to fail. This is unfortunate. In my view, the essential enterprise of schooling is students and teachers learning together.[4] The grading process needs to be turned away from serving what many students see as the essential enterprise of their time in school and toward the goal of in-depth learning. As this chapter's "From the Classroom" example illustrates, grades can be tools to hold students responsible for knowing history *and* being able to do history.

HERE I STAND: YOUR EXPERIENCE WITH GRADES

❖ *What resources are available to you that can help you learn about grading and evaluation practices?*

❖ *Have your grading practices changed much over the years you have been teaching? What would be a good example?*

❖ *In your classroom, do you use grades*

_____ to check what history kids have learned?
_____ as a motivational tool?
_____ to satisfy external requirements, like transcript analysis for college admissions?
_____ to satisfy parents', guardians', or students' questions?
_____ to mold the student learning process you want (for example, increasing collaboration)?
_____ to help kids focus on their learning styles?
_____ to make curriculum and evaluation seamless?
_____ to teach kids higher-level thinking skills?
_____ other uses?

Can you offer an actual example from your teaching that is tied to one of these categories?

❖ *Do you have other comments about evaluation and grading that you would like to add?*

FROM THE CLASSROOM: RELIGION IN THE SCHOOLS

Our planned objectives for "Using Stories to Learn About Religion, Using Religion to Learn About Life," the classroom example for this chapter, were 1) to introduce students to Islam, Christianity, and Judaism, the three major religions studied in their Western Civilization course; and 2) to provide students with entry-level practice in using primary sources, including reading, analyzing, writing, and revising, within a collaborative setting. For primary sources on Western religions we excerpted six biblical stories, two from each of the Holy Books of the three religions. From the Koran we took the story of Adam and Eve and a poetic vision of the End of Time. From the New Testament we included the stories of the Prodigal Son and the Good Samaritan. And from the Torah we chose the stories of Abraham and the Sacrifice of His Son, Isaac, and David and Goliath.

For our involvement activity we intended to emphasize the story aspect of these primary sources. Stories, after all, can tell truths that sometimes cannot be spoken more directly. Many believers find more meaning in tales than in doctrinal statements. That, we would suggest to the students, is why, historically, religions have used stories to reveal fundamental insights—sometimes mysterious secrets—about what it means to live "the good life." We planned to point out that these primary sources from the sacred texts of Islam, Christianity, and Judaism not only teach us something about the basic tenets of the three religions, they also offer valuable advice that has survived the test of centuries.

We hoped ferreting out these hidden meanings would be appealing to middle and high schoolers as long as we did not push the "valuable-advice-from-adults" message too hard. Perhaps their study of history would contribute to their development as they grew into young adults and, in turn, that their developmental needs might pump energy into their historical study of Western religions.

The effectiveness of the unit's opening involvement activity relied, unfortunately, on a terrible coincidence. We had scheduled the first lesson of the project (in a class that included ninth, tenth, eleventh, and twelfth graders) for what turned out to be the Monday after the weekend shooting death, at home, of a student in the school. Just about everyone in school that morning knew of the shooting, but some were more upset than others. I learned later in the day that one young woman in our class was the mother of the dead man's child, and another was his close friend. Both were in class that Monday morning.

It was more than a so-called "teachable moment." It would have been downright cruel to ignore the students' pain and upset. We had planned to "hook" the kids into the historical primary sources by holding out the lure of their usefulness. Now, standing before students who were confronting a true life crisis, we found ourselves explaining how stories, religious stories in particular, can be used to help yourself through a difficult time. When a friend dies, we told the class (hoping we were being helpful), feelings are aroused. These feelings often include grief and sadness as well as anger and fear. When the friend is as young as you are, it can make you wonder about big questions, questions so overwhelming that sometimes stories offer more help than a direct dialogue. Or, stories can lead to a dialogue.

Heeding our own advice, we briefly introduced the six stories, offering along the way a few words on language, transliteration, and the origin of each religion. The students needed an overview so that they could decide which story they would like to work with. We asked them not to choose one they were already familiar with, a proscription that was, however, not universally followed.

Several of the stories are reprinted here as examples of the sources the students read and analyzed. They are not quickly read and dispatched. On the contrary, they present complicated and sometimes upsetting messages that are worth thinking about, especially after a traumatic event.

❖ ❖ ❖ ❖ ❖ ❖ ❖ ❖ ❖

"The Story of the End of Time"
(*from the Koran*)

When the sun shall be darkened,
when the stars shall be thrown down,
when the mountains shall be set moving,
when the pregnant camels shall be neglected,
when the savage beasts shall be mustered,
when the seas shall be set boiling,
when the souls shall be coupled,

when the buried infant shall be asked for what sin she was slain,
when the scrolls shall be unrolled,
when the heavens shall be stripped off,
when Hell shall be set blazing,
when Paradise shall be brought nigh,
then shall a soul know what it has produced.

❖ ❖ ❖ ❖ ❖ ❖ ❖ ❖ ❖

"The Story of Abraham and the Sacrifice of his Son Isaac"
(from the Torah)

. . . Some time afterward, God put Abraham to the test. He said to him, "Abraham," and he answered, "Here I am." And He said, "Take your son, your favored one, Isaac, whom you love, and go to the land of Moriah, and offer him there as a burnt offering on one of the heights that I will point out to you." So early next morning, Abraham saddled his ass and took with him two of his servants and his son Isaac. He split the wood for the burnt offering, and he set out for the place of which God had told him. On the third day Abraham looked up and saw the place from afar. Then Abraham said to his servants, "You stay here with the ass. The boy and I will go up there; we will worship and we will return to you."

Abraham took the wood for the burnt offering and put it on his son Isaac. He himself took the firestone and the knife; and the two walked off together. Then Isaac said to his father Abraham, "Father!" And he answered, "Yes, my son." And he said, "Here are the firestone and the wood; but where is the sheep for the burnt offering?" And Abraham said, "God will see to the sheep for His burnt offering, my son." And the two of them walked on together.

They arrived at the place of which God had told him. Abraham built an altar there; he laid out the wood; he bound his son Isaac; he laid him on the altar, on top of the wood. And Abraham picked up the knife to slay his son. Than an angel of the Lord called to him from heaven: "Abraham! Abraham!" And he answered, "Here I am." And he said, "Do not raise your hand against the boy, or do anything to him. For now I know that you fear God, since you have not withheld your son, your favored one, from Me." . . .

The students' work with these sources was organized so that everyone shared in generating questions and in determining personally satisfying *and* valid (our definition of "correct") answers. As soon as the class had been divided into collaborative groups and the groups had sat down together, each student chose one of the six stories. There were two restrictions on freedom of choice: the story had to be new to the student and each student in the group had to have a different story. That way, a collaborative group of four, for example, would have access to four sources.

The structure for the project followed a classic "jigsaw" pattern. To achieve this collaboration, we divided the work for the unit into five steps.

Each student began by reading his or her own story. Since the kids were sitting in groups facing one another, they could and sometimes did share ideas that interested them, express puzzlement aloud, or ask other students or the teachers for help. After reading the story, each student then rewrote it in his or her own words.

As the worksheet in Figure 5–1 shows, there is a teacher Check Point here. No one could continue to the next step unless a teacher had checked the paraphrased version of the biblical tale and agreed that the student's retelling adequately and accurately captured the plot, the main characters, and the principal events. *Depth* comprehension and inner meaning were not yet at issue. That would be a task for the group to deal with later, collaboratively. At the Check Point we wanted only to ensure that when students read, told, or showed their stories to their partners, who had not read them, what was passed on was a valid rendition. Otherwise, the expert might be unknowingly misleading other students.

After all the students in the group had successfully navigated the Check Point, each student took a turn telling the others in the group the story he or she had read and rewritten. That process often became a dialogue as students asked one another questions, expressed their opinions, and took notes. Once everyone had heard and understood all the stories, the group moved to a more general discussion about what could be learned from them. The search for meaning was guided by the two questions listed on the worksheet and discussed with the class: What do these stories from the Koran, the New Testament and the Torah tell you about the way the world is? What advice do they give, explicit or implied, about how a "good" person should live his or her life?

At first glance it might seem that, just as in a traditional classroom, the teachers had generated the questions the students were to answer. In fact, however, these "test" questions were the result of an enterprise shared between students and teachers. And because they were so broad—almost unanswerable—the *actual* questions the students addressed in their group discussions and the writing assignment that followed were generated by the students themselves. For example, one group of students asked, Can you have confidence in yourself even though you are a small person and don't act "big"? And, Can you always know who the "bad" people in the world are?

Finally, when the group had finished the discussion or the teachers said time was up, whichever came first, each student wrote his or her own version of what the group had concluded, from their primary sources, about the advice the three western religions offered them. As usual, they had to substantiate their statements, ideas, and conclusions with specific references to the group's (limited) "data pool."

FIG. 5–1: Worksheet: Using Stories to Learn About Religion

Your name: _____

You will work in a group of three or four students. Each student will have <u>one</u> of the following stories:

The Story of Adam and Eve in the Garden of Eden *(Koran)*
The Story of the Good Samaritan *(New Testament)*
The Story of Abraham and the Sacrifice of his Son Isaac *(Torah)*
The Story of the Prodigal Son *(New Testament)*
The Story of the End of Time *(Koran)*
The Story of David and Goliath *(Torah)*

Step One: Read your story. (Ask the teachers or someone else in your group for help with words and ideas you have trouble with.)

Step Two: When you are sure you understand your story, rewrite the story here in your own words. (Who are the main characters? What happened? Why?)

Check Point: Get a teacher's initials here before continuing._____

Step Three: Tell (or read) your story <u>in your own words</u> to the other people in your group.

Step Four: Have a group discussion to decide what the stories tell you about what the
world is like and how you should live in it.
Before you begin the discussion choose a Facilitator. The job of the Facilitator is to
make sure everyone participates in the discussion.
Our group's Facilitator is _____

Step Five: When you feel you've learned all you can from each other's stories, each
person is to write up the group's conclusions. Your written answer should have:
a. an opening paragraph which states the group's main conclusions.
b. a middle section which gives more information and more details—like examples
from the stories. EVERY CONCLUSION MUST BE BACKED UP BY A REFERENCE
TO ONE OF THE STORIES!
c. a final paragraph which pulls together everything in your essay <u>or</u> makes a new
point based on what you wrote.

**Everybody's essay will be collected, read, and returned with comments and a grade. One
essay from your group will also be chosen as the group's sample essay. Your grade will be
an average of the grade your essay gets and the grade of the sample essay.**

*The reason for this is to encourage you all to work together and help each other learn.
In unity there is strength—and learning!*

❖ *Do you agree that teachers and students together shared in generating the questions students had to answer? Do you have a comment to add?*

WHY SCAFFOLDING IS MORE IMPORTANT THAN WHAT IS GRADED

For this Western Civilization history project there was little difference between how grades were determined (the "test") and how learning happened (the project). In other words, to describe the project is to describe the evaluation process, including giving grades.

Let us return to the classroom example.

As the worksheet explains, the grade for the unit was simply an average of the grade on the individual essay and the grade on the sample essay chosen by the teacher. (The criteria for evaluating the essay are listed in Step Five.) But that makes it sound as if the essays were the only work that was graded and evaluated. Couldn't a savvy student skim the stories and whip off an "A" essay, or have someone else write it for him at home? We need to back up and ask another question: What was needed to write a "good" essay? When we examine that question we will know what the grading "system" encouraged, discouraged, and evaluated.

Because of the project's scaffolding, a student could not, as in a traditional class, read four or five primary sources on his own and write a paper. On the contrary, to finish the graded essay, each student had to

- be in a collaborative group (given the project's structure, the only way to have access to the stories was to belong to a collaborative group)
- choose a primary source that no one else in the group had chosen
- read and understand the source well enough to paraphrase it in writing (Check Point)
- present the plot, main characters, and details of the story to the group in a way the other students could understand
- understand the stories the others in the group presented when it was their turn
- participate in a general discussion about what could be learned from these stories (Some students were silent during the discussions, taking from others rather than contributing. Most students, however, wanted to participate. The discussions, after all, raised challenging questions of special interest to them.)
- write an essay that depends on, and includes, the thinking of the group as a whole (Collaboration can turn "cheating" on its head for students, so that learning from one another is something positive

rather than the desperate act of a kid who feels—and probably is—out of it.)
- accept the need for collaboration and revision as a basic part of the learning process

The essay was the product of a series of collaborations, each of which prompted students to revise their thinking. In other words, from start to finish, revising and rethinking were structured into how learning took place. Each student began by understanding one story and then added several others to his or her repertoire as they were presented through the eyes of other students. Each student discussed and debated the questions raised by the sources with peers and argued over which questions the group should focus on. Again, students brought multiple perspectives to bear. Checking their analysis and tentative hypotheses against the primary sources, students further readjusted their thinking. They also revised their essays during the writing process.

Each student's essay was the end product of a collaborative learning process. To grade the essay was to encourage that process.

> ❖ *In your opinion, did the* grading structure *for this unit encourage and reinforce the growth of higher-level thinking?*
>
> *For example, did it*
>
> > *reward students who generated significant or interesting questions in partnership with other students and their teachers?*
> > *reward students for working collaboratively with classmates?*
> > *reward students for creating hypotheses that could be validated by an analysis of the primary sources they worked with?*
> > *reward students for presenting their conclusions in writing?*
> > *reward students for accepting cooperation and revision as necessary to the development of conclusions?*

GRADING IS NOT MY FAVORITE PART OF TEACHING

I want to ask readers to do a short grading exercise. That way we can turn the theoretical even more toward the concrete. What follows is a sample essay written by a ninth grader for the "Religion" unit. Read this essay as if you were the student's teacher. See Step Five of the student worksheet for the evaluation criteria that guided the student in his writing.

From looking at all the stories I can say that the world is like this: the world is full of signs, and not just signs, but meaningful signs, signs that make a statement and also tell us why things are the way they are. Also that we shouldn't take stuff for granted and that you may never know who is the bad person in the world. Also we should always have confidence in yourself and just because you are small it doesn't mean you still can't act big. Also we should spend some time wondering what we have done wrong.

The reason why I say that the world is full of signs is because it is like what is told in "The End of Time." Also the reason why I say "we shouldn't take stuff for granted" is because you never know when you'll lose it as in "Adam and Eve." Also, the reason why I say that you should have confidence in yourself is because if you let someone bully you, you'll never be strong. You'll always be weak as in the story of David and Goliath. Also when I say the world is full of sinfulness and not everyone comes back from being sinful as happens in "The Prodigal Son."

I say that all the statements are true because you should be a little of all of what I said. If you're not, then at least you should have learned a little of what I said.

❖ *What grade would you give the student?*

❖ *What comments would you make?*

❖ *Would you require a rewrite?*

❖ *To the extent that you can tell from the information provided here, does the essay show that the student's work included higher-level thinking?*

　Were the questions tackled generated by the student, and do they seem original to him (however banal they might seem to others)?
　Do the questions stem from his work with the primary sources assigned?
　Were his ideas validated by references to the primary sources assigned?
　Does the essay show that his learning process was collaborative?
　Does the essay show that revisions were made, either in forming ideas or in the writing itself?

　Do you have additional comments?

WHERE ARE YOU NOW?

❖ *Are you satisfied with how you grade?*

❖ *What is one thing that you took from this chapter that you might use now in your classroom?*

❖ *What problems that are important to you as a teacher were not mentioned here?*

NOTES

1. See Joseph P. McDonald et al., *Graduation by Exhibition: Assessing Genuine Achievement* (Alexandria, VA: ASCD, 1993); Grant P. Wiggins, *Assessing Student Performance: Exploring the Purpose and Limits of Testing* (San Francisco, CA: Jossey-Bass, 1993).

2. For a more detailed discussion of the role of objectivity and accuracy in the teaching and writing of history, see Chapter 6.

3. National Center for History in the Schools, *National Standards for United States History*, University of California, Los Angeles, pp. 66–67.

4. I heard David Green use this language at a Coalition of Essential Schools presentation in Providence, Rhode Island, Oct. 14, 1993.

6

Let the Future Write the Past

We believe that the chief value of curriculum revision does not lie in the product made, but in the process of the making. In the construction of the courses of study the outstanding benefit has been the rekindling of the intellectual life of all those who have participated in the enterprise.

Senior high school curriculum guide,
Long Beach City Schools,
Long Beach, CA, 1937

THE PLACE BETWEEN

What is a history "curriculum"?

Nowadays much of the country's attention seems to be centered on those whose answer is "the history that all students ought to know." There has been a concerted effort to define for all schools what is to be included in a "course of study." Organizations like the National Center for History in the Schools, based at UCLA, and the National Council for History Education (formerly the Bradley Commission on History), to choose two examples, have gathered prominent historians and educators together to define the content and skills students should learn in each history course. The politically controversial National History Standards is one instance of their work.[1]

Those responsible for the standards and their more conservative critics love history and take it seriously. The first concern of both of these folks is *what* is learned: they care about how kids learn, but their primary focus is on history as subject matter. It is through our common heritage, they believe, our shared national past, that this nation of diverse peoples has remained united and democratic. Without a common curriculum we could revert to what some have called "tribalism."

There are other historians, teachers and educators,[2] however, who would dispute that defining the "right" history is the only approach to curriculum revision or to promoting national unity. Those who take a different perspective, like the curriculum developers in Long Beach, California, back in 1937, whose words open this chapter, care about content but focus first on the learning experiences of the students and the teachers who are studying history. They spotlight how learning takes place in schools and pay close attention to the *process* by which children learn. Their goal is to gain greater clarity in understanding the variety of ways history can be taught and learned in schools. They know that what is taught matters. Yet for many of these folks, the surest guarantee of a united and democratic nation is a thoughtful, caring citizenry whose study of history helps them to think deeply and critically.

History teachers need a varied repertoire of teaching methods so that they can choose the ones that best match their goals and objectives for their students. Still, the focus on achieving a consensus on what history should be mastered seems strange to me, even "unteacherly," as if the proponents of the primarily-"content" approach understand more about history than about what happens in middle and high schools. Experienced teachers can easily distinguish between the "curriculum on paper" and what actually occurs in class. Nor is it a secret to either classroom practitioners or education researchers how much content students forget between one test and the next. Why put your best energy into making content lists that do not differ greatly from recent textbooks?

I believe history teachers—and teacher educators—need to consider how our students learn and do not learn, whether we are talking about students who lack academic English and a middle-class background and thus *appear* less academically able, or students working diligently in honors classes.

To begin with, we know that what kids learn may or may not be what teachers think they are teaching. Teachers are reminded by classroom experience—too often for their own comfort—that the connection between teaching and learning is neither simple nor direct. "Good" teaching does not always lead to the expected outcome. You can plan carefully, execute to perfection, do everything just right, yet what you present or "cover" is not necessarily what students learn. At the extreme, students may break the learning "connection" completely and decide to shut down, no matter what the personal consequences. Sometimes entire classes never come together in ways that permit continuous attention to the curriculum. The difficulties can be schoolwide. Two of the schools in which we worked had a daily absentee rate above twenty-five percent as well as a significant transient student population. That made it more difficult to sustain a sense of community in the classroom, or to build continuity and develop skills over the course of the year. In many school districts today, those conditions are the facts of life.

Learning is a highly individualized process that includes emotional as well as cognitive elements. How it occurs varies widely among students. I would argue that serious, in-depth learning, including deep understanding of "factual" content, often takes place in the "space" between the teacher's or the textbook's words, on the one hand, and the individual student's way of thinking about things, on the other hand. That gap—the intellectual and emotional space between teachers and students—is important. It gives kids leeway to struggle for themselves with what they encounter in a classroom. If we want the history curriculum to move beyond mere memory of surface material, we should set up classes so that, at least some of the time, students are given responsibility for "fighting" with the material.[3] Otherwise, the history we teach will go in one ear and out the other and lack a life beyond the classroom.

The history students learn in middle and high school classrooms is not so easily determined by hardworking experts laboring outside those classrooms. For better or worse, students have more control over the curriculum they actually learn than content-oriented curriculum planners seem to realize. It is what happens in classrooms—between students and teachers and between students and students—that matters most. That is why I wish curriculum planners would focus more on *how* learning history occurs, and less on prescribing what material should be included in the textbook and course syllabus.

HERE I STAND: YOUR EXPERIENCE WITH CURRICULUM DEVELOPMENT

❖ *When you think about the history curriculum today, do you see two camps, one emphasizing the selection of content, the other principally concerned with how students learn history?*

❖ *What are your thoughts about my contention that, for better or worse, students have more "control" over the history they learn than many curriculum planners give them credit for?*

❖ *If you were invited to join in the creation of a new United States history curriculum (salary is negotiable!) what are the three most important problems you would like your group to tackle?*

A STUDENT HISTORIAN'S GUIDEBOOK:
WHOSE COUNTRY IS IT, ANYWAY?

What might a course of study look like if it focused on how students learn history rather than on the content such a course should include? Would it be very different from what most teachers are now accustomed to?

It would be a mistake to underestimate how difficult teaching history would be without a textbook or textlike materials. Textbooks provide a "skeleton" on which daily work can be based. They keep kids focused on the chronology that, with rare exceptions, the course must cover.

Yet it is these very benefits that can make existing texts an impediment for those who want to focus on *how* students learn. What makes a textbook so helpful to teachers and students is the narrative chronology, which appears to be an accurate and objective re-creation of the past. Even texts that include alternative perspectives, primary sources, and debates among historians present what purport to be reliable summaries of historical events. Thus, the very presence of a good textbook—a readable and accurate history narrative—can suggest to students that when studying history they need not venture very far beyond the textbook.

Despite the obvious usefulness of the traditional textbook, however, there are better ways to study history. What if we replaced the textbook, whose heart is a chronological narrative, with a guidebook for teachers (and students) using documents and primary sources extensively in their classes? Given the demands on students, teachers, and schools, a student historian's "textbook" that focused on the student's *process* of learning would have to meet three (somewhat contradictory) criteria to be practical and usable:

- allow students to raise their own questions and make their own decisions about historical definitions ("What is history?") and interpretations
- help students learn content by teaching them how to be a community of practicing student historians, capable of analyzing, synthesizing, and validating, who construct history themselves
- include a way to learn the *core content* usually found in traditional narrative textbooks and assessed on standardized tests

What might such a "textbook" look like? Let us take U.S. history as a case in point. As usual, since we expect energy and self-discipline from our students, we start with student involvement. Because few school-age people are persuaded for long when teachers tell them what to think or feel, the student historian's book would begin by drawing students into complex stories of people their own age. I imagine it opening with stories about (fictional) students who have apparently taken this same U.S. history class in an earlier year in a school similar to their own. The characters in the stories are three-dimensional; they have a life outside of school, relations with other kids, and clear, if changing, feelings about the teacher and the job at hand. The stories emphasize the students' point of view: mixed feelings about their new class, and their frustration and confusion about what is expected of them.

Their new guidebook would include several sets of opening stories. Teachers and students would select those whose central characters match their own self-defined characteristics; for example, grade level, neighborhood, gender, aspirations, and ethnic, racial, or religious background. This would not only facilitate student identification with the fictional models in the stories, it would also give students from diverse backgrounds the green light to think of U.S. history as their history, a notion that might seem strange to a number of them.

Let us say, for example, that our text is being used in a school with a student population as rich and diverse as the population of the United States itself. The class has decided to start with the conventional period 1763–1775. The first story in the set of opening stories is about a young man who wishes he were in the Advanced Placement U.S. history class. Why he wants to be in the AP class has nothing to do with curriculum or textbooks. He met two guys who are in the AP class when he tried out for the basketball team. (One of them says he is getting a bright blue Mazda Miata for his sixteenth birthday.) Now that they have all been cut, the three of them hang out a lot together. Also, while he does not actually have a girlfriend, he is madly in love, and has been since the first day of school, with a young woman he would see much more often if he were in AP history with her. His essay for the period 1763–1775 is titled, "They Made the Revolution Happen: Advertising and Propaganda in a Mass Movement." His time line includes the Boston "Massacre" (he puts it in quotes), the formation of the Sons of Liberty, the tar and feathering of Stamp Act tax collectors, the Declaration of Independence, and the publication of Tom Paine's *Common Sense*. His essay is upbeat. He sees public relations as necessary for any mass movement. Otherwise, he asks, how would people's opinions ever change? He pictures Sam Adams as an organizational genius, with a finger directly on the people's pulse. Adams, Paine, and Jefferson knew how to make things happen. If alive now, they would quickly adapt and be successes in twentieth-century politics—or television. His historical map is two face-to-face diagrams, one of the actual Boston "Massacre" and the other a version publicized throughout the colonies by that genius Sam Adams.

The central character in the second story is a young woman from Haiti who has been in the United States for a year and a half. She lives with her mother, three sisters, and a younger brother. Her father and oldest brother are still in Haiti, where they work in a family business with her uncle and grandfather. Her father has been saying for over a year he will join them "very soon." But the young woman does not understand this; she no longer believes what her father writes. She is worried and very angry. She wishes she could talk to someone official about her situation before she and her sisters' student visas expire. Her mother will make no phone calls and insists on speaking French at home. Her essay was originally titled "The Indians Were Lied To and Cheated," but the day before she handed it in, her peer editing partner convinced her to change the title. Her time line for "The Wars Against the Indians" includes Pontiac's Rebellion, the Paxton Boys' rebellion and march on Philadelphia, the "Regulators" in North Carolina, and the war against the Shawnees in Virginia. Her historical map, which she has drawn in vibrant colors, shows the locations of the British forts west of the Appalachians, all but three of which were attacked and destroyed by Pontiac. Her essay is short and sad to read. Her mother is upset with her for writing about such things in school.

The third and final story in the opening set is about two young women, best friends, both from Mexican-American families, who work together as partners. They met in Model Legislature in the eighth grade. That year they cochaired three successful car wash projects to raise money for a class trip to Washington, D.C. Their theme is, "Women and Children." They had trouble with their time line because, as one of them said in her self-evaluation letter, "Nothing big happened like an event we could point to." Instead, on their time line they included dates of excerpts from a diary, dates of baptisms and deaths taken from church records, the date of a Franciscan monk's letter calling for the conversion of "heathens" and the building of mission-forts, and the date of a sermon on the dangers to Christians of "native" women working as servants (reprinted as a broadside). Their essay lacks analysis; it is almost entirely descriptive. It includes anecdotes about women with their families in what is now New Mexico. Their historical "map" is a diagram of a typical southwestern church mission of the period.

These three stories share a common "plot" line: In each one, students are asked to write an account of a brief chronological period in the history of what is now the United States; each student approaches the past in a highly personalized way that corresponds to current needs and values; and it turns out okay. Woven into each story are the student's time line, a short essay written by the student, and a historically accurate map drawn by the student. The ten to fifteen "events" on the time line are the primary evidence the student historian offers to substantiate his or her interpretive theme. The brief essay begins by stating that theme and then describes it using people and events from the time line as supporting documentation.

The historical map highlights whatever the student historian decides to emphasize.

These opening stories in our imagined book involve the students in a process intended to transform them from traditional students of history into student historians. They highlight some of the perplexing dilemmas that lie at the heart of studying and writing history. What are we to make of three different, contradictory, and exclusive interpretations, all substantiated by references to historical "facts"? Is one history more "correct" than the others? Can there be more than one correct history? Do students have the right to use the past for their own purposes? These are questions, our guidebook is suggesting, that should be faced and discussed in class.

What follows in the guidebook is a second set of stories. These stories also have an ambitious teaching and learning agenda. They raise questions about exactly what constitutes historical evidence, and where and how to find it. In other words, how are conclusions and generalizations validated? Like the first group of stories, they are told from the student's point of view, they are complicated and concrete, and they include three parts—a theme, an essay describing that theme, and a map.

What is missing this time around, however, is the time line with its supporting evidence. It falls to the students in the class to choose one of the essay interpretations and with the teacher's help and direction to supply ten to fifteen events that could support the fictional student's interpretation. When students unearth appropriate supporting data successfully, they add it to the time line and rewrite the essay to include documentation.

How will kids find the information they need? For most middle and high school students, using research libraries to track down primary and secondary materials would be an insurmountable problem, even if they worked collaboratively. Fortunately, in addition to anthologies of printed documents, commercially prepared and reasonably priced U.S. history data base programs are available through hypercard technology, some on disks, others on CD-ROM, and still others on the Internet.[4]

Working from a disc, a student might begin by selecting from a list of chronological periods, topics, or other items of interest. A new menu would appear, inviting the user to choose from subcategories like literature, political history, fine arts, demography, urban history, black history, foreign policy, or education; or from a range of primary sources, like speeches, newspaper accounts, still pictures, movie clips, diary excerpts, maps, graphs, poems, paintings, folk songs, and other artifacts, as well as historians' interpretations. For most programs, all the student needs to do is to "click" on the icon. Teachers and students can manipulate the available data, add to the data base, or create entirely new programs of their own.

Once the kids are relatively comfortable with the skills and ways of thinking necessary to find supporting evidence and with their inherent right to be student historians, the next step is to put together what they have learned so far. There are no stories in this third section of the text. Instead there are lists of diverse themes for several chronological periods; sample primary sources, documents, and other artifacts; and lists of "core content" examples (the people, events, and movements that typically appear in traditional narrative textbooks). Students browse through the sample sources to decide on a theme and then move to the hypercard data base to find support from the past. They arrange the evidence they have discovered on a time line. They write essays describing the theme and documenting it with examples from the time line. Finally, they deal with the core content examples.

Given the diverse interests of students and the variety of available sources and documents, especially when strict content restraints are dropped, most of the usual core content examples would probably not be used in students' own histories. In those cases, student historians would be required to explain why they omitted the core content examples and whether that information contradicts their interpretation. In this way, much of the traditional core content of U.S. history would be "bootlegged in": students with nontraditional interpretations would have to learn traditional history (the core content examples) in order to explain why they have the right to omit them. And by being involved in discovering their "own" past within the nation's history (and getting support in the classroom for doing so), students will find the energy to learn the core content normally "covered" in a traditional course at least as well as most students in more traditional courses do.

Like any textbook, a student historian's guidebook would be simply a starting place. Teachers and students would have considerable autonomy about how to proceed. Much depends on what the teacher decides to emphasize and on what puzzles or interests the kids. The bulk of the student historian's text would consist of material usually found in the teacher's edition of a traditional textbook but also helpful to students. "It's My Country, Too" (the working title for the student historian guidebook) should include several versions of possible periodization schemes for U.S. history, each with its own justification; sample student theme essays with marginal notes critiquing strengths and suggesting improvements; guidelines for creating historical maps; examples of historical maps with notes about why, for whom, and how those particular maps are useful; examples of themes that transcend chronological periods; core content examples cross-listed by chronological period and topic; student historian "practice" projects that raise specific process problems (for example, working with primary sources that contain dramatic internal contradictions or include complex values issues); test items for the core content examples; a bibliography of interesting, diverse, and accessible films, filmstrips, videos, software programs, CD-

ROMs, and lesser known sources (for example, architectural drawings, demographic tables, picture histories of people at work, youth archives); lists of resource organizations; and stories by (fictional) students about having the power of the historian in their own hands.

Teachers and students choose what is useful as they make their way through their own chronologies, interpretations, and definitions of the history of what is now the United States. Discussions, role playing, or journal writing based on the first stories, for example, could help kids understand what it means when student historians draw different conclusions about the "same" reality. Days, or even weeks, could be spent on projects designed to tease out the political, philosophical, and methodological issues embedded in these opening stories, depending on the time available. Is one account more acceptable than the others? Is one more powerful? Why do these histories differ? Are such questions best answered individually or by a community? Do we need to know the history of history writing?

Learning about historical evidence and how it is used to validate interpretations—the issues raised by the second set of stories—would also require considerable classwork. In my experience, most students do not realize how complicated asking questions, either of people or of documents, can be. They must learn through practice with primary sources how to deal with ethnocentric biases, how to uncover internal evidence that might give clues about intention, point of view, or fabrication, and how to untangle "fact" and "opinion." The text provides primary source projects that raise these questions and discrete exercises and skill-building activities for those who want them.

The third section of the guidebook—putting it all together—is designed to help students learn a broad range of thinking skills over the course of the year. The guidebook emphasizes problem solving and critical thinking. When successful, users of such a text would come to understand, through their own experience working collaboratively with sources, documents, and artifacts, that all critiques of necessity include personal perspectives and individual values. The guidebook would help student historians understand what it means to validate conclusions using appropriate evidence. The text would also ask students to practice basic functional writing. After all, they need to comprehend what a theme is and how a theme can organize an essay.

❖ *Does the textbook determine the history "curriculum"?*

❖ *Would using a student historian's guidebook like the one described here change the way you taught? How?*

❖ *Would using a student historian's guidebook change the way your students learned? How?*

❖ *Would you try a textbook without a narrative chronology if one were available now?*[5]

LET THE FUTURE WRITE THE PAST

Bias and Objectivity

With or without the support of a helpful guidebook, being a student historian consists of more than mastering skills. Historians' goals include reproducing as accurately as possible validated accounts of what happened in the past. Should we accept what students write as "accurate" history that is worth studying? Or, is the gap between what middle and high school students can do and the work of highly trained and experienced professionals unbridgeable?

Certainly student historians are biased. I would go even further: they glory in their bias. It is what makes their study of history important to them. The student historian approach *urges* young people to read sources and write history from their own perspective. Being personally involved with their sources is the teacher-recommended procedure. That is how the students find the energy to care, and that is the source for the insights that make the students' written accounts seem "genuine" to them. On top of that, student historians, steeped in their own development, tend to be a parochial, mercurial group. Some adults in schools would argue that adolescence is a built-in bias. And, finally, these young historians will not be free to roam libraries and archives sampling the available sources. That means even students whose classrooms are equipped with CD-ROM databases and Internet access work from a preselected collection of sources.

But are student historians as a group any more biased than other historians, including trained professionals? The term "bias" has highly negative connotations, and with good reason. Too often it is associated with prejudice and discrimination. But bias and prejudice are not synonymous. To be biased means to have a perspective, a frame of reference, a particular point of view. Everyone has a perspective: we see the world through our own eyes, heart, and mind. To be human is to experience life through a personal frame of reference. Every perspective, then, is biased in the sense that it represents one person's vision. Therefore, to be human is to be, well, biased.

Strange as it may seem, historians need to be biased. Without this personal perspective history could not be written. Bias gives form to accounts of the past. All of life cannot, after all, be replicated on paper (or even digitally). Without a point of view, historians would sail rudderless through a morass of equally meaningless—or meaningful—data, unable to make sense of the overwhelming, buzzing, booming confusion they encounter in source materials. As they work, historians must make choices. A point of view guides, and limits, the selection of sources as well as the analysis of sources. The topics, patterns, themes, people, and events—the historical chronologies and narrative accounts we have come to accept as "The Past"—are all reflections of the decisions of historians about what is worthy and significant. Without each historian's individual bias (whether we agree or disagree with the account) nothing that makes sense to the rest of us would ever be written.

To be objective, then, does not mean to lack bias. That is impossible. Nor is it, as some would argue, a matter of professional detachment, as if the worker had no interest in his work! Hearing "both sides" of an issue—a popular definition of "objectivity" in school classrooms—assumes that all questions can and should be reduced to two opposing viewpoints. Most questions are much more complicated.

I think of objectivity as a learning and study process rather than as the absence of personal perspective. As a process, objectivity requires working according to a set of rules that make clear to yourself, and to those who follow and check your steps, how you worked and why you decided what you did. It means sharing and acknowledging premises and assumptions; utilizing known pools of evidence; not ignoring what you know, or could know, including the work of others in your field; and being clear about your criteria for drawing conclusions based on shared evidence. That is the best a person can do.

A Checkpoint Interlude

❖ *Do you agree that as a teacher-historian your perspective ("bias") determines what you consider to be significant history, that is, history that is worth studying? Do you have a comment on this question?*

❖ *In your opinion, which topic is more truly worthy of study, the causes of the War Between the States, or changes in knitting styles during the first half of the nineteenth century?*

_____ Causes of war   _____ Changes in knitting

What personal perspective ("bias") does your choice reflect? Are all those who disagree with you wrong or just different? Who says so?

Climate and Synthesis

Since I walk to work regularly I have a great interest in weather and climate. Climate is an "average" of the weather over time at a certain place, an average with predictive value. As an example, take the average temperature for each day in January in my home city, Providence, Rhode Island, over the last fifty years. Compute the average of those temperatures and you have a numerical description of the midwinter climate in Providence. It is accurate enough for me to decide how warm a jacket I will need next January.

But despite its predictive value, it is still an illusion.

Climate is only a meaningful synthesis about the weather when we purposely limit the data that is available. Use *all* the information we have, and climate disappears. It is no longer possible to determine an average! What is the average January temperature for that spot on earth now known as Providence, Rhode Island, if we look not just at the last five decades but at the last five million years? We can come up with a number. But it will describe neither a typical "January" during the Ice Age nor a typical January in the twentieth century. (Actually, there is sufficient temperature variation within this century that even by expanding our view to one hundred years we start to lose meaning. Bodies of water that once froze regularly in the region now no longer do so.) Because we have different distributions—the Ice Age and the twentieth century—in our average, the problem is unsolvable. There is a southern New England climate only when we limit the information included in our study to the data that can be synthesized into an average that seems *meaningful* to us. To talk about climate, we must act as if most of what we know, or could know, does not exist.

The problem is similar, and equally unsolvable, for historians who want to develop a historical synthesis for a certain time and place in the past. The textbook approach to history assumes that to have learned about, say, the Renaissance, or the French Revolution, or the Gilded Age, is to have learned about Italy in the fourteenth and fifteenth centuries, France in the second half of the eighteenth century, and the United States in the latter part of the nineteenth century. Actually, what historians—highly skilled, well intentioned, hard working historians—have done is to isolate and then focus on only those data that feed into the "average" they feel best describes the period under study. This is the historian's task. If a historian tried to synthesize "all" the daily events, ideas, actions, conflicts, creations, relationships, work, and play that were important to those alive during that time period, they—and we—would wind up with chaos.

Of course there are accepted syntheses, like the Renaissance, that have stood the test of time and are worthy of study. Many interesting and valid syntheses that reflect a particular historian's perspective ("bias") help us understand the past. Students ought to know about them. But to value what we have is different from claiming accuracy in fully reconstructing a time period as it was. The latter, for better or worse, is a false hope.

I ask your openness to the idea that new, useful, and interesting historical accounts can be created by today's student historians precisely because they bring their own youthful earnestness and diverse perspectives to their study of sources. I ask you to accept that the next generation has the right to measure, probe, and evaluate. Like all other historians, students writing history bring to the past their particular perspective. Like all other historians, students must face directly questions of bias and objectivity. Like all other historians, students work with and cite limited sources, concentrating on those that support their "synthesis." But unlike other historians, middle and high school students who write history add to our understanding of the past something valuable that was previously missing: the focus of the rising generation.

When the "histories" a class writes are placed together, they form neither chaos nor, obviously, a new synthesis but a mosaic. As long as students follow the general guidelines required of all historians, the *results* can be valuable as history: interesting, enlightening, worthy of study, valid. Let the future write the past.

NOTES

1. The National History Standards are available from the National Center for History in the Schools, UCLA, 10880 Wilshire Blvd., Los Angeles, CA 90024; "History Matters!" is published by the National Council for History Education, Inc., 26915 Westwood Rd., Suite B-2, Westlake, OH 44145.

2. See, among many others, the works of historians like Peter Stearns, Russell Hvolbek, Robert Berkhofer, John Anthony Scott, Carl Becker, Tom Holt; and teachers and educators like John Duffy, Ed Abbott, Ted Sizer, Jerome Bruner, Jacqueline Brooks, Edwin Fenton, Robert Kuklis, and James Banks.

3. The responsibility for how these thoughts are phrased is my own, but I am grateful for conversations on these subjects with my colleague Tom James.

4. Examples include CD-ROMs like Voyager's *Who Built America?*, Primary Source Media's *American Journey: History in Your Hands* series, and discs (with hypercard technology) like Scholastic's *Civil War*. According to the *Washington Post* (Oct. 10, 1994), both the National Archives and the Library of Congress plan digitized publication projects of parts of their holdings, available either as CD-ROMs or on the "information highway."

5. For textbooks with only a limited chronological narrative, see Irving Bartlett, Edwin Fenton, David Fowler, and Seymour Mandelbaum, *A New History of the United States: An Inquiry Approach* (New York: Holt, Rinehart and Winston, 1969); Richard N. Current and Gerald J. Goodwin, *A History of the United States* (New York: Alfred A. Knopf, 1980); Allan O. Kownslar and Donald B. Frizzle, *Discovering American History* (New York: Holt, Rinehart and Winston, 1967); see also, Bert Bower, Jim Lobdell, and Lee Swenson, *History Alive! Engaging All Learners in the Diverse Classroom* (Menlo Park, CA: Addison Wesley, 1994), for a book that stresses diverse learning styles in the teaching of history.

Postscript

The "histories" student historians create by working collaboratively have value. They are a fortunate outcome of the student historian approach. But the histories themselves are *secondary* benefits. They are not the principal reason for using documents and other primary sources to teach and learn history. The main purpose of the student historian approach is not, after all, to produce a nation of historians. As history teachers our first goal is always to educate as best we can the young people given temporarily into our care.

Some historians and history teachers worry about approaches to the study of history that encourage diversity in defining the past. Without traditional survey courses, standard textbooks, and a common curriculum they fear that the rising generation may well lack a sense of shared community, that the United States could devolve into a nation of hostile and competing groups.

I believe that the bond that holds us together is more complicated: *how* students learn as well as *what* they learn determine their growth. Above all, it is their ability to pose pertinent questions, define problems, analyze relevant information, support their conclusions, and understand their own values—their ability to think, care and know—that will insure students' growth into thoughtful, responsible citizens in a thoughtful, democratic community. Such an approach to schooling, guaranteed to all students, is, I believe, our future's greatest safeguard and a teacher's most serious responsibility.

What postscript or other final comments would you write for *Beyond the Textbook: Teaching History Using Documents and Primary Sources*? Copies of your comments can be sent to the author at: Education Department, Brown University, Box 1938, Providence, RI 02912.

The author and publisher wish to thank those who have generously given permission to reprint borrowed material:

"Hermaphrodites as Laborers" and "Indians Hunting Deer" on pp. 25 and 26, courtesy of the John Carter Brown Library at Brown University.

"Lorenzo de' Medici" by Andrea del Verrocchio on p. 41, Samuel H. Kress Collection, © 1995 Board of Trustees, National Gallery of Art, Washington.

"Pietà" by Michelangelo Buonarroti on p. 47 from Alinari/Art Resource, NY.

Excerpt from *The Prince* by Machiavelli from *The Shaping of Western Society: An Inquiry Approach* by John M. Good, copyright © 1968 by Holt, Rinehart and Winston, Inc., reprinted by permission of the publisher.

"A Letter Home" from *Dear America: Letters Home From Vietnam*, edited by Bernard Edelman for the New York Vietnam Veterans Memorial Commission. Copyright © 1989. Published by Simon & Schuster Inc. Reprinted by permission of the author and editor.

"Testimony of Former Corporal Daniel J. Evans" from *A New History of the United States, an Inquiry Approach* by Irving Bartlett, Edwin Fenton, David Fowler, and Seymour Mandelbaum, copyright © 1975 by Holt, Rinehart and Winston, Inc., reprinted by permission of the publisher.

Excerpts from *I Saw Them Die, Diary and Recollections of Shirley Millard* by Adele Comandini, reprinted by permission of Harcourt Brace & Company.